arihant
SUCCESS AND NOTHING LESS

AF819906

Be a TOP SCORER
in ICSE Exams 2025

i Succeed

10 Sample Question Papers

with Quick Study Notes

Literature in English 10th
Paper 2

AUTHOR
Pritika Singhal

Arihant Prakashan
(School Division Series)

Administrative & Production Offices

Regd. Office
'Ramchhaya' 4577/15, Agarwal Road, Darya Ganj, New Delhi -110002
Tele: 011- 47630600, 43518550

Head Office
Kalindi, TP Nagar, Meerut (UP) - 250002
Tel: 0121-7156203, 7156204

Sales & Support Offices
Agra, Ahmedabad, Bengaluru, Bareilly, Chennai, Delhi, Guwahati, Hyderabad, Jaipur, Jhansi, Kolkata, Lucknow, Nagpur & Pune.

PRICE ₹165.00

PO No : TXT-59-T060593-8-24

Published by Arihant Publications (India) Ltd.

For further information about the books published by Arihant, log on to www.arihantbooks.com or e-mail at info@arihantbooks.com

Follow us on

i Succeed

SAMPLE QUESTION PAPERS

THE **BEST CHOICE** OF TEACHERS & STUDENTS, Why?

01 Exact Exam Pattern

All Sample Papers have been designed on the actual exam format of ICSE

02 Complete Syllabus

Complete coverage of syllabus through different types of questions across all the sample papers

03 Latest Specimen Question Paper

Latest Specimen Question Paper with detailed answers.

04 Detailed Answers

Step-by-step answers to help you understand concepts and improve problem-solving skills.

05 Quick Study Notes

Focused revision of the whole syllabus through Quick Study Notes.

06 All Type of Questions

Coverage of all type of exam pattern questions, recall, analysis, understanding, application & evaluation

With Free
DOUBT SOLVING APP

Free Doubt Solving APP

To help you sort out your doubts at any time any place.

i Succeed

English Literature 10

Course Structure

2024-25

There will be one paper of two hours duration of 80 marks and Internal Assessment of practical work carrying 20 marks.

I. **DRAMA: Julius Caesar: William Shakespeare (Acts III, IV & V)**

II. **TREASURE CHEST: A Collection of ICSE Short Stories & Poems (Evergreen Publications (India) Ltd. New Delhi)**

PROSE (Short Stories):

1. With the Photographer – Stephen Leacock
2. The Elevator – William Sleator
3. The Girl Who Can – Ama Ata Aidoo
4. The Pedestrian – Ray Bradbury
5. The Last Lesson – Alphonse Daudet

POETRY:

1. Haunted Houses – H.W. Longfellow
2. The Glove and the Lions – Leigh Hunt
3. When Great Trees Fall – Maya Angelou
4. A Considerable Speck – Robert Frost
5. The Power of Music – Sukumar Ray

NOTE: The ICSE (Class X) Examination paper will be set ONLY on the portion of the syllabus that is prescribed for Class X.

Preparation Assessment Zone

Welcome to the Preparation Assessment Zone !

In this section, you'll find **ICSE Specimen Question Paper** to help you assess your readiness.
Attempt this paper to familiarize yourself with the exam format and identify areas that need improvement.

Progress Tracker Tick the papers as you complete them.

☐ ICSE Specimen Question Paper

ICSE Specimen Paper 2025

Session 2024-25

Literature in English 10th (Code 01)

General Instructions

1. You will not be allowed to write during the first 15 minutes. This time is to be spent in reading the question paper.
2. The time given at the head of this paper is the time allowed for writing the answers.
3. The paper has four sections.
4. Section A is compulsory - All questions in Section A must be answered.
5. You must attempt one question from each of the Sections B, C and D and one other question from any section of your choice.
6. The intended marks for questions or parts of questions are given in brackets [ ].

- No. of Questions : 7
- No. of Sections : 4
- Time Alloted : 2 Hrs.
- Max. Marks : 80

Section A (Attempt all questions from this section)

Question 1. (16)

Choose the correct answer to the questions from the given options.
(Do not copy the question, write the correct answers only.)

(i) Where was Caesar put to death? [Recall]

(a) On a street in Rome (b) On the battleground of Philippi
(c) At the foot of Pompey's statue (d) In Brutus' orchard

(ii) Who asks permission to speak at Caesar's funeral? [Recall]

(a) Brutus (b) Antony
(c) Cassius (d) Octavius

(iii) "Woe to the hand that shed this costly blood! Over thy wounds now do I prophesy..." These lines tell us that Antony is......... . [Analysis]

(a) enraged (b) sorrowful
(c) anxious (d) frustrated

(iv) When Antony says, 'This is a slight unmeritable man, / Meet to be sent on errands', he refers to [Recall]

(a) Lepidus (b) Octavius
(c) Pindarus (d) Lucilius

(v) What strategy does Cassius suggest that the conspirators follow? [Understanding]

(a) March towards Philippi (b) Remain where they are
(c) Raise an army of foot soldiers (d) Set fire to the surrounding villages

(vi) When Cassius says, 'My life is run his compass', he means that......... . **[Understanding]**

(a) it is the day on which Brutus was born
(b) his life had come full circle
(c) his life could be measured with a compass
(d) his life could be compared to a race

(vii) Which of the given options contains the figure of speech that appears in the following line from Leigh Hunt's poem 'The Glove and the Lions': 'Ramped and roared the lions'? **[Application]**

(a) 'Your eyes are like the diamond bright',
(b) 'Suddenly the black night showed its teeth in a flash of lightning'.
(c) 'Rich gifts of raiment or grain or gold'?
(d) 'Pack up the moon and dismantle the sun'.

(viii) Which of the following is not an effect of Bhishma Lochan Sharma's powerful singing in Sukumar Ray's poem 'The Power of Music'? **[Understanding]**

(a) The sky weeps tears
(b) The trees shake and crash
(c) The people retire amazed
(d) The turtles whine and stare

(ix) Which of the following words does H. W. Longfellow use to describe the movement of the phantoms in his poem 'Haunted Houses'? **[Recall]**

(a) Slide
(b) Glide
(c) Noiseless
(d) Invisible

(x) The theme of Maya Angelou's poem 'When Great Trees fall' is .... **[Analysis]**

(a) the impact of the death of a loved one on those left behind
(b) the effect of felling trees on the environment
(c) how the death of trees affects humanity
(d) the impact of natural calamities on a forest

(xi) The poem 'A Considerable Speck', captures .... **[Understanding]**

(a) the journey of a mite across a sheet of paper
(b) the poet's determination to kill the mite
(c) the poet's encounter with a gigantic fly
(d) the mite's attempt to escape from the fly

(xii) In Stephen Leacock's 'With the Photographer', while waiting for the photographer, the narrator spent time .... **[Recall]**

(a) examining the studio
(b) talking on his phone
(c) writing in his diary
(d) reading magazines

(xiii) In Ama Ata Aidoo's short story 'The Girl Who Can', Nana expressed her disapproval of Adjoa's legs because .... **[Understanding]**

(a) they were slender
(b) they were muscular
(c) they were bent
(d) they were short

(xiv) Choose the option that lists the sequence of events from Alphonse Daudet's short story 'The Last Lesson' in the correct order. **[Understanding]**

I. But, when he arrived at school, Franz was dismayed to find his classmates already seated quietly and solemnly in their places ...... and shocked when M. Hamel simply urged him to take his place.

II. Franz hurried to school that morning he was very late and dreaded being scolded by M. Hamel, the teacher.

III. After he had settled at his desk, he noticed something really odd: the back benches of the classroom were occupied by adults from the village!

IV. He hoped to slip into the classroom unnoticed, under cover of the bustle and noise of a typical school day morning.

(a) I, III, II and IV
(b) II, IV, I and III
(c) III, I, IV and II
(d) IV, II, III and I

(xv) Select the option that shows the correct relationship between Statements (I) and (II) from William Sleator's short story 'The Elevator'. [Analysis]

Statement I Terrified of the fat lady in the elevator, Martin ran down the dark stairs, fell and broke his leg.

Statement II Angry and disappointed that his son had behaved like a fool and a coward, Martin's father did not talk to him on the way to the hospital.

(a) (I) is true and (II) is false.
(b) (II) is true and (I) is false.
(c) (I) is the cause for (II).
(d) (I) and (II) are independent of each other.

(xvi) Ray Bradbury's short story 'The Pedestrian', can be best described as .... [Evaluative]

(a) utopian
(b) dystopian
(c) humorous
(d) a fairy tale

Section B (Answer one or more questions from this section)

DRAMA

Julius Caesar

By William Shakespeare

Question 2.

Read the extract given below and answer the questions that follow.

Caesar : Are we all ready? What is now amiss,
That Caesar and his Senate must redress?

Metellus : Most high, most mighty, and most puissant Caesar,
Metellus Cimber throws before thy seat
A humble heart, ... [He kneels]

(i) Where are the speakers?
What does 'puissant' mean?
Explain: 'Metellus Cimber throws before thy seat a humble heart'. [Recall and Understanding] (3)

(ii) At the beginning of the scene, Caesar says, 'The Ides of March are come.'
Why do you think Caesar said this?
What does the Soothsayer say in response? [Recall and Understanding] (3)

(iii) What specific duties do the conspirators allot to Trebonius and Casca?
Why does Cassius become nervous when Popilius Lena speaks to him as they enter? [Recall and Understanding] (3)

(iv) What does Artemidorus want of Caesar?
How does Caesar respond to his plea? [Recall] (3)

(v) Shortly after this exchange, Caesar is stabbed to death by the conspirators. Whom do you sympathise with Julius Caesar or the conspirators? Give reasons for your choice. [Evaluative and Analysis] (4)

Question 3

Read the extract given below and answer the questions that follow.

Brutus : I did send to you
For certain sums of gold, which you denied me;

For I can raise no money by vile means:
By heaven, I had rather coin my heart,
And drop my blood for drachmas, than to wring
From the hard hands of peasants their vile trash
By any indirection.

(i) To whom are these words addressed?
Why is Brutus angry with this person? **[Recall and Understanding] (3)**

(ii) How does this person feel when he hears these words?
What does he say to defend himself? **[Analysis and Recall] (3)**

(iii) Why did Brutus need 'certain sums of gold'?
Why was he unable to raise these sums of money? **[Understanding] (3)**

(iv) Earlier in this scene, Brutus refers to Lucius Pella.
What had he been accused of?
Who had supported him and how? **[Recall] (3)**

(v) Mention any two aspects of Brutus' character that are revealed in the above extract.
What do you understand about the relationship between Brutus and the person he addresses? **[Analysis] (4)**

Section C (Answer one or more questions from this section)

PROSE-SHORT STORIES

(Treasure Chest-A Collection of ICSE Short Stories and Poems)

Question 4.

Read the following extract from Stephen Leacock's short story 'With the Photographer' and answer the questions that follow.

"The photographer beckoned me in. I thought he seemed quieter and graver than before. I think, too, there was a certain pride in his manner.

He unfolded the proof of a large photograph, and we both looked at it in silence.

'Is it me'? I asked.

'Yes', 'he said quietly, 'it is you', and we went on looking at it.

(i) Where was the narrator?
Why had he gone there?
Why do you think that there was a certain pride in the photographer's manner? **[Recall and Understanding] (3)**

(ii) What does the word 'proof' mean in this context?
Why did the narrator ask, 'Is it me'? **[Understanding] (3)**

(iii) Which of the narrator's facial features had the photographer altered? **[Recall] (3)**

(iv) What was the only part of the narrator's face that seemed original in the photograph?
How did the photographer plan to 'fix' this? **[Recall] (3)**

(v) At the end of the story, the narrator flies into a rage.
What makes him angry?
How would you justify the narrator's angry outburst? **[Understanding and Analysis] (4)**

Question 5

Read the following extract from Ray Bradbury's short story 'The Pedestrian' and answer the questions that follow.

"He would stand upon the corner of an intersection and peer down long moonlit avenues of sidewalk in four directions, deciding which way to go, but it really made no difference;"

(i) What was Leonard Mead's occupation?
What did he love to do?
When is the story set? **[Recall, Understanding and Recall] (3)**

(ii) To what does Mead compare his walk through the empty streets?
Mention two reasons he gives for making this comparison. **[Recall and Understanding] (3)**

(iii) Why had Mead decided to change his footwear from hard-heeled shoes to sneakers? **[Understanding] (3)**

(iv) What happened quite suddenly as he was making his way home?
What was Mead's immediate reaction? **[Recall] (3)**

(v) Why was Mead taken away by the police car?
Would you call this a horror story or a piece of science fiction? **[Understanding and Analysis] (4)**
Give reasons for your answer.

Section D (Answer one or more questions from this section)

POETRY

(Treasure Chest - A Collection of ICSE Short Stories and Poems)

Question 6.

Read the following extract from H.W. Longfellow's poem 'Haunted Houses' and answer the questions that follow.

The stranger at my fireside cannot see
The forms I see, nor hear the sounds I hear;
He but perceives what is; while unto me
All that has been is visible and clear.

(i) What makes the poet-narrator different from the stranger at his fireside? **[Understanding] (3)**

(ii) According to the poet, what turns a house into a haunted house? **[Understanding] (3)**

(iii) Where is one likely to meet the 'phantoms' in a haunted house? **[Recall] (3)**

(iv) What are the poet-narrator's views on owning property? **[Recall and Understanding] (3)**

(v) How do the poet's views of ghosts differ from the traditional perception of ghosts? How would you describe the mood that the poem evokes? Give one reason for your answer. **[Understanding and Analysis] (4)**

Question 7.

Read the following extract from Maya Angelou's poem 'When Great Trees Fall' and answer the questions that follow.

When great trees fall in forests, small things recoil into silence, their senses eroded beyond fear.

(i) What effect does the falling of a 'great tree' have on the creatures of the forest? **[Recall and Understanding] (3)**

(ii) How does the death of a great soul affect the lives of those left behind in the immediate aftermath of their passing? **[Understanding] (3)**

(iii) What long-term effect does the death of a 'great soul' have? **[Understanding] (3)**

(iv) What feeling is being expressed by the following lines/phrases? **[Analysis] (3)**

(a) Small things recoil into silence

(b) Kind words/ unsaid,

(c) be and be/ better. For they existed

(v) What is a 'Great tree' a metaphor for?

What is the central message of Angelou's poem, 'When Great Trees Fall'? **[Application and Analysis] (4)**

Answers in Topper's Style

1. (i) (c) At the foot of Pompey's statue

(ii) (b) Antony

(iii) (a) enraged

(iv) (a) Lepidus

(v) (b) Remain where they are

(vi) (b) his life had come full circle

(vii) (c) 'Rich gifts of raiment or grain or gold'?

(viii) (d) The turtles whine and stare

(ix) (b) Glide

(x) (a) the impact of the death of a loved one on those left behind

(xi) (a) the journey of a mite across a sheet of paper

(xii) (d) reading magazines

(xiii) (a) they were slender

(xiv) (b) II, IV, I and III

(xv) (c) I is the cause for II.

(xvi) (b) dystopian

2. (i) The speakers are at the Capitol in Rome, sitting at the Senate.

The word 'puissant' means having great power or influence.

The line 'Metellus Cimber throws before thy seat a humble heart' means that Metellus Cimber requests Caesar to listen to his plea with a humble heart.

(ii) Previous to the given conversation, the Soothsayer had warned Caesar about the ides of march as he predicted a threat around Caesar on that day. Caesar had dismissed his concerns.

Caesar had said the above line to remind the Soothsayer that it was already ides of march and he was unharmed.

The Soothsayer in response reminds him that the day is not over yet.

(iii) Trebonius was given the task to lure Antony out of the Senate room so that Caesar is left alone with the conspirators. Casca was asked to be the first to attack and stab Caesar.

Before entering the Senate room, Popillius Lena wishes Cassius good luck for his enterprise that day. Hearing his commendation, Cassius becomes nervous as he thinks Lena has discovered the conspirators' plans to assassinate Caesar.

(iv) Artemidorus requests Caesar to address his letter as a matter of priority. He tries to entice Caesar into opening his letter first by informing Caesar that the contents of his letter pertain to Caesar directly.

Caesar refuses to open Artemidorus' letter. He decides to address any personal matters last as he wanted to address the matters of his people and subjects first. He establishes that the welfare of his people comes before his own.

(v) Based on the above short exchange, I sympathise with Caesar. He was not a perfect leader but he was a good and strong ruler.

He refused to read Artemidorus' letter as it addressed a personal issue. Instead, he insisted on reading matters of his people first. This shows his dedication and concern for his subjects over his own. He valued the welfare of his people over his own.

He was a just and stern ruler who upheld law and order above everything else. Even after several pleas from Metellus Cimber and other conspirators to allow Metellus's brother, Publius to return to Rome, Caesar refuses as Publius was banished by lawful means. This shows Caesar's honour and fair-mindedness.

Caesar was also known to share wealth with the poor. He redistributed land to the poor and soldiers. His will stated to share some part of his wealth among the poor after his death.

Being such a fair and powerful leader for Rome, he didn't deserve to be murdered by the hands of the conspirators, some that he considered friends.

3. (i) Brutus is addressing the above words to Cassius.

Brutus is expressing his anger and disappointment after learning that Cassius was accepting bribes in exchange of power. He also expresses his frustration when Cassius refused to send him money when he needed it.

(ii) Cassius felt angry and hurt after hearing Brutus's accusations.

He defends himself by clarifying that he didn't intend to refuse help. Instead, the messengers had made a mistake and caused a miscommunication between them.

(iii) Brutus needed the money to help pay the soldiers of his battalion.

He was unable to gather such a sum as he didn't have any funds of his own and refused to raise money using vile means. He argues that he would rather turn his own heart into gold and his blood drops into silver coins than rob poor and innocent villagers of their hard-earned money.

(iv) Lucius Pella was accused of siphoning off money from the Sardians. Brutus humiliated Pella by condemning his actions and disgraced him.

Cassius had written to Brutus defending Pella and requesting him to absolve Pella of these accusations. He says so because he knew the man well.

(v) The above extract showcases Brutus's high morals. He holds honesty and loyalty on the highest pedestal and expects others to do the same. In the extract, Brutus condemns Cassius for accepting bribes. He expresses his disappointment in Cassius for committing such a shameful act.

However, this scene also showcases the double standards. As he criticises Cassius's act of accepting bribes, he also argues with Cassius for not aiding him financially to pay his battalion using the bribe money. By doing this, he establishes that he can never extort money from the poor but doesn't mind using Cassius's 'loot' to pay his soldiers.

The relationship between Cassius and Brutus is shown to be strained in the above dialogue. They quarrel and find faults in each other without accepting their own mistakes. It showcases evident differences in their personalities and value system that leads to clashes between them.

4. (i) The narrator was at the Photographer's studio.

The narrator went to the studio to get a picture of him clicked. He wanted to get a good picture of him to serve as a memory for his friends and loved ones when he dies.

As the narrator's looks were not ideal or 'good' according to the photographer, he struggled with taking a good picture of the narrator. So, the photographer was proud of his work as, according to him, he was able to produce a 'good' picture of the narrator despite the narrator's bad features.

(ii) The 'proof' in the above extract means the sample or draft of a picture before it is finally printed.

The narrator enquired if the person in the picture was him as he could not recognise himself. The photographer had edited and distorted the image a lot and the narrator struggled to find any resemblance between him and the person in the picture.

(iii) The photographer had altered the narrator's eyes, eyebrows, forehead, facial hair, and mouth.

(iv) The only part of the narrator that seemed original in the photograph was his ears.

The photographer planned to use a new technique called Sulphide to remove the ears entirely in the final edit to 'fix' them.

(v) The narrator was furious as the picture didn't look like him at all. The photographer had altered his appearance to match his own superficial standards.

The narrator is justified in his angry outburst. The photographer was unprofessional and insensitive to the narrator's feelings. The narrator simply wanted an image of his own. Instead, he got humiliated and body shamed by the photographer. Initially, the narrator was extremely amiable and patient to the photographer's criticism. He tried to amend himself as much as possible. However, the photographer's constant degrading remarks about his features had a negative impact on his self-worth and image, and eventually pushed him to fury.

5. (i) Leonard Mead was a writer by profession.

He loved to go out for long evening walks every day to get some fresh air after all his neighbours had retired inside their homes to watch television. The story is set in 2053 A.D.

(ii) Mr. Mead compares his walk in the vacant streets to the shadow of a hawk in the Arizona desert.

He makes the comparison as the roads were empty and deserted in his neighbourhood in the evening. He only saw some dogs and had his own thoughts for company. The emptiness of the streets reminded him of his home.

Being the only person out on the streets, he feels lonely and singled out. He feels like a hawk in the Arizona desert looking for civilisation.

(iii) Mr. Mead decided to change his footwear from heels to sneakers to avoid confrontations with the street dogs. His boots had hard heels which would make sound when he walked on concrete or pavement. This would gather the attention of the stray dogs who would chase after him. So, to avoid making loud noises to alert the attention of the stray dogs, he shifted to sneakers which would make a softer noise.

(iv) Mr. Mead saw a lone car turning around the corner. The car turned out to be the only police car out for patrolling.

Mr. Mead was surprised to see the car as he was not expecting anyone to be on the streets at that hour of the day. He knew that most people in the society were glued on their couch watching television shows at that time of the day.

(v) Mr. Mead was taken away by the police car for walking aimlessly around the town late in the evening.

I would call the story a piece of science fiction. The story sheds a light on the dangers of overdependence on technology in today's world. With new advancements, most manual jobs have been replaced by machines. Technology has made work simpler, faster and more efficient. However, it also led to people becoming lazy and addicted.

In the world that Bradbury describes, the society is technologically-ruled. People are addicted to television and human interactions have become minimal. The crime rates have gone down so only one AI controlled cop car is used to patrol the whole city at night.

Mr. Mead, the protagonist, is the symbol of soul and humanity by not conforming to this new norm. Through his story, Bradbury tries to display an admonishing tale which warns the world of the disadvantages of becoming technologically driven. He predicts that such a society would mean a loss of individuality, creativity and autonomy. He prompts the need to strike the right balance between technology and human experiences for a better life.

6. (i) The poet is different from the stranger at his fireside as the stranger can only feel the presence of people they could see around them. Whereas, the poet can see and hear the ghosts as well. He also suggests that the stranger can only see the present while the poet has the ability to also perceive the past.

(ii) The presence of the phantoms of people who used to live or died in the houses made the house 'haunted', according to the poet.

(iii) One can meet the 'phantoms' anywhere in the house. They can be found gliding around the house through the doors. We can meet them at the doorways, on the stairs or along the passages and halls of the house.

(iv) The poet believes that the living people in the houses don't own the houses or lands they inhabit. He states that the spirits who lived in these houses and lands are the original owners of those lands. They hold deeds to the houses in their hands, reaching their hands out of their graves.

(v) Traditionally, the presence of ghosts in a house or land is considered to be a frightful ordeal. Most people believe that ghosts are vengeful spirits that haunt the earth because of unfinished business or spite. However, the poet paints a harmless image of the ghosts in the poem. He believes that the ghosts are gentle and keep to themselves. They have no intention of disturbing the living and want to coexist with them in harmony.

The poem tries to invoke the mood of security and comfort. Throughout the poem, the poet ensures the presence of phantoms in the house or around us is not malevolent. He constantly paints the image of the ghosts going about their day completing their own errands. For instance, at dinner parties, they crowd around the dinner table and hall, enjoying the festivities without any interference. Their involvement in the event is as much as of the pictures that hang around the walls, silent and observing.

7. (i) When 'great trees' fall, the effect is felt in the whole forest. The loud noise frightens mighty animals like lions and elephants. Lions hunker down into tall grasses and elephants lumber to seek safety. Small animals also recoil into their places of safety till the vibrations die down.

(ii) After the loss of a great soul, the lives of the people they leave behind changes tremendously. In the initial days of grief, the air around them feels thin and rare. They find difficulty in breathing. They are overwhelmed by the hurtful reality of the absence of their loved one. They are flooded by their memories and guidance that helped them progress in life. They are consumed with remorse for kind words that were left unsaid or promises that were never fulfilled.

(iii) In the long term, our reality is forever plagued by the memory of the 'great soul'. Our souls that once flourished under the guidance of the 'great soul' start to shrink and shrivel from their absence. We struggle to cope with the emotional void we feel after they leave. The impact is so immense that sometimes we start to question our existence without them. We feel lonely and isolate ourselves from others to cope up with our grief.

(iv) The feeling being expressed in the given.

(a) Feelings of shock and panic

(b) Feeling of regret

(c) Feeling of optimism and bittersweet hope

(v) The 'great tree' is a metaphor for a great soul or significantly wise personality in our life. An old tree provides food and shelter to many small or big animals in a forest. When it falls, the entire forest is shocked and stunned by its loss. The animals who depended on it for food and shelter, don't have its protection now. It leaves a visibly large void where it stood, and the animals dependent on it have to eventually look for another way of survival.

Similarly, the poet uses the metaphor 'great tree' to emphasise on the loss of a loved one in our life and how their sudden absence impacts us. Our loved ones provide an environment of love and support. They guide us and help us learn the ways of life. But, their sudden demise is traumatic for us. The loss of their protection leaves us feeling clueless and helpless. Their absence leaves a void in our life which cannot be filled very easily. But eventually we heal and move on. Their memory and influence linger behind and help us shape our lives positively.

Proficiency Building Zone

Welcome to the Proficiency Building Zone !

This section contains **10 Sample Question Papers** designed to enhance your problem-solving skills and proficiency. Use these papers to practice regularly and track your progress. Remember, consistent practice is key to mastering Literature in English.

Progress Tracker Tick the papers as you complete them.

- ☐ Sample Paper 1 _____ (Fill your score)
- ☐ Sample Paper 2 _____ (Fill your score)
- ☐ Sample Paper 3 _____ (Fill your score)
- ☐ Sample Paper 4 _____ (Fill your score)
- ☐ Sample Paper 5 _____ (Fill your score)
- ☐ Sample Paper 6 _____ (Fill your score)
- ☐ Sample Paper 7 _____ (Fill your score)
- ☐ Sample Paper 8 _____ (Fill your score)
- ☐ Sample Paper 9 _____ (Fill your score)
- ☐ Sample Paper 10 _____ (Fill your score)

SQP Code : **PB-1/10** Series *i*-**Succeed 1-25/10** Roll No. | | | | | | | | |

Sample Question Paper 01

Literature in English 10th (Code 01)

General Instructions

1. You will not be allowed to write during the first 15 minutes. This time is to be spent in reading the question paper.
2. The time given at the head of this paper is the time allowed for writing the answers.
3. The paper has four Sections.
4. Section A is compulsory - All questions in Section A must be answered.
5. You must attempt one question from each of the Sections B, C and D and one other question from any section of your choice.
6. The intended marks for questions or parts of questions are given in brackets [ ].

Time : 2 Hrs.

Max. Marks : 80

Section A (Attempt all questions from this Section)

Question 1.

Choose the correct answer to the question from the given options. (16)

(i) What does Lucilius feel about Cassius welcome? [Analysis]

(a) Cassius was hurt by Brutus's actions.
(b) Cassius was not as friendly as before.
(c) Cassius was full of regret for his actions.
(d) Cassius was eager to meet Lucilius.

(ii) Why does the crowd want to tear Cinna, the Poet apart even after knowing he is not a conspirator? [Recall]

(a) For having the same name as the conspirator. (b) For not believing his claims.
(c) For being outside during riots. (d) For being a bad poet.

(iii) What is the meaning of the following lines [Understanding]

"Shall ever take alive the noble Brutus:
The gods defend him from so great a shame"!

(a) Brutus should never suffer the indignity of being a captive.
(b) Brutus should never be called a coward.
(c) Brutus should never get to know how his friends died.
(d) Brutus should never know the shame of being a traitor.

(iv) Which of the following lines is an example of irony? [Application]

(a) And men are flesh and blood, and apprehensive;

(b) I do know but one that unassailable holds on his rank,

(c) Ambition's debt is paid

(d) I could be well mov'd, if I were as you;

(v) "In such a time as this it is not meet
That every nice offence should bear his comment".

Characteristic of Cassius was showcased in the above lines is ……… . [Understanding]

(a) his pragmatism (b) his egoism

(c) his militarism (d) his patriotism

(vi) Who does Brutus think he has offended? [Recall]

(a) Those who love Rome. (b) Those who are friends of Caesar.

(c) Those who wish to be slaves. (d) Those who are ambitious in life.

(vii) In H.W. Longfellow's 'Haunted Houses', what were the ghosts at the table compared to? [Understanding]

(a) Photographs on the wall (b) Strangers

(c) Furniture (d) Earthly mists

(viii) What does the poem 'When Great Trees fall' illustrate? [Understanding]

(a) Beauty of Nature (b) Importance of forests

(c) Dangers animals face in the forests (d) Impact of Death and Grief

(ix) What is the fate of the mite that the poet decides in 'A Considerable Speck'? [Understanding]

(a) Let it lie and sleep (b) Crush it under his pen

(c) Chase it away from the paper (d) Trap it and throw it out

(x) In the poem 'The Glove and the Lions', why did the lady drop her glove in the arena? [Recall]

(a) She wanted to prove that her lover was braver than the King.

(b) She wanted to feed her lover to the lions and marry the King.

(c) She wanted to test her love and gain everyone's attention.

(d) She wanted to see what the lions would do with her glove.

SP-01

(xi) In 'The Power of Music', the poetic device used in the line 'the feathered fly turn turtle' is [Understanding]

(a) Metaphor (b) Simile

(c) Hyperbole (d) Alliteration

(xii) In Ama Ata Aidoo's short story 'The Girl Who Can', how did Maami react to Adjoa's victory? [Understanding]

(a) She picked up her daughter and kissed her. (b) She scolded her daughter for participating.

(c) She distributed sweets to her neighbours. (d) None of these

(xiii) Why was Mr. Mead's profession a threat to the society in Ray Bradbury's short story 'The Pedestrian'? [Recall]

(a) He was a writer so he was creative and had individuality.

(b) He was a writer so he would always live in a fantasy world.

(c) He was a writer so he was poor and homeless.

(d) He was an actor so he was creative and had individuality.

(xiv) In 'With the Photographer', the narrator did not read .... [Recall]

(a) Girls Magazine
(b) Politics Today
(c) Ladies Companion
(d) Infants Journal

(xv) Select the option that shows the correct relationship between Statements (I) and (II) from Alphonse Daudet's short story 'The Last Lesson'. [Analysis]

Statement I The bulletin board said that only German would be taught in schools of Alsace.

Statement II M. Hamel was planning to leave France the next day.

(a) I is true and II is false.
(b) II is true and I is false.
(c) I is the cause for II.
(d) I and II are independent of each other.

(xvi) Choose the option that lists the sequence of events from William Sleator's short story 'The Elevator' in the correct order. [Recall]

I. Martin climbs the elevator coming back from school.
II. Martin falls down the stairs.
III. Martin tells his father about the lady.
IV. Fat lady climbs the elevator to the Third floor.

(a) III, II, I and IV
(b) I, IV, III and II
(c) I, IV, II and III
(d) I, III, IV and II

Section B (Answer one or more questions from this Section)

DRAMA

Julius Caesar

By William Shakespeare

Question 2.

Read the extract given below and answer the questions that follow.

Artemidorus : O Caesar, read mine first; for mine's a suit
That touches Caesar nearer: read it, great Caesar.

Caesar : What touches us ourself shall be last served.

(i) How is Artemidorus feeling in the above line?
Give reason for Artemidorus' feelings.
Does his worry get resolved? [Recall and Understanding] (3)

(ii) How does Artemidorus plead with Caesar?
What is the significance of the word 'suit' here? [Recall and Understanding] (3)

(iii) How does Caesar respond to Artemidorus' appeal?
What does his reaction tell us about Caesar? [Recall and Understanding] (3)

(iv) Do you agree that Caesar was being stubborn in the above extract? Give reasons justifying your answer. [Evaluative and Analyis] (3)

(v) Explain the line : "What touches us ourself shall be last served."
Can you say that this line depicts a split between his public and private self? [Evaluative and Analyis] (4)

Question 3.

Read the extract given below and answer the questions that follow.

Cassius : I an itching palm?
You know that you are Brutus that speak this,
Or, by the gods, this speech were else your last.
Brutus : The name of Cassius honours this corruption,
And chastisement doth therefore hide his head.
Cassius : Chastisement!
Brutus : Remember March, the ides of March remember:
Did not great Julius bleed for justice' sake?
What villain touch'd his body, that did stab,
And not for justice? What, shall one of us
That struck the foremost man of all this world
But for supporting robbers, shall we now
Contaminate our fingers with base bribes,
And sell the mighty space of our large honours
For so much trash as may be grasped thus?
I had rather be a dog and bay the moon,
Than such a Roman.

(i) What does 'an itching palm' mean here?
Why does Brutus use the phrase? [Recall and Understanding] (3)

(ii) What happened on ides of March?
Why does Brutus remind Cassius of it? [Recall and Understanding] (3)

(iii) How does Cassius feel when he hears Brutus' words?
How does he defend himself? [Recall and Understanding] (3)

(iv) Did Brutus feel that Cassius was acting like Caesar? Why?
What does Brutus say he would rather be than being a dishonest Roman?
[Evaluative and Analysis] (3)

SP-01

(v) What was Brutus's main argument against Cassius that led to the above dialogue?
Why had Brutus not taken any action against Cassius yet? [Evaluative and Analysis] (4)

Section C (Answer one or more questions from this Section)

PROSE-SHORT STORIES

(Treasure Chest - A Collection of ICSE Short Stories and Poems)

Question 4.

Read the following extract from Stephen Leacock's short story 'With the Photographer' and answer the questions that follow.

"This is my face. It is not yours, it is mine. I've lived with it for forty years and I know its faults. I know it's out of drawing. I know it wasn't made for me, but it's my face, the only one I have-" I was conscious of a break in my voice but I went on- "such as it is, I've learned to love it. And this is my mouth, not yours. These ears are mine, and if your machine is too narrow-" Here I started to rise from the seat.

Snick!

(i) Who is saying the lines in the above extract and to whom?

What is he/she feeling?

How old is the speaker of these lines? [Recall and Understanding] (3)

(ii) Why was the narrator angry?

Was he justified in his feelings? [Recall and Understading] (3)

(iii) How was the photograph taken in the end? [Recall and Understanding] (3)

(iv) What did the narrator explain to the photographer?

Do you think the photographer understood what he said? [Recall and Understanding] (3)

(v) Did the narrator seek the photographer's approval?

Why? [Evaluative and Analysis] (4)

Question 5.

Read the following extract from William Sleator's short story 'The Elevator' and answer the questions that follow.

"The stairs were no better. Martin tried them one day after school. There were no windows, and the lights were not working. Martin's footsteps echoed behind him on the cement, as though there was another person climbing, getting closer. By the time he reached his home on the seventeenth floor, he was gasping for breath.

Martin's father worked at home. He wanted to know why Martin was out of breath. "Why didn't you take the elevator?" he asked, frowning at Martin. You're not only skinny and weak and bad at sports, his face seemed to say, but you are also a coward. After that, Martin always took the elevator. He would have to get used to it, he told himself, just like he got used to being bullied at school".

(i) Why was Martin's father at home?

What did he ask Martin?

Pick out the word in the above extract that expresses his feelings about Martin's response. [Recall and Understanding] (3)

(ii) Why did Martin not like climbing the stairs?

How many floors did Martin climb to reach home? [Recall and Understanding] (3)

(iii) What did Martin perceive from the looks his father gave him? [Recall and Understanding] (3)

SP-01

(iv) Did Martin take the elevator the next time?

Why did he decide to do so? [Evaluative and Analysis] (3)

(v) Martin was not able to tell his father about his problems. Why?

What does this say about his father? [Analysis and Understanding] (4)

Section D (Answer one or more questions from this Section)

POETRY

(Treasure Chest - A Collection of ICSE Short Stories and Poems)

Question 6.

Read the following extract from Leigh Hunt's poem 'The Glove and the Lions' and answer the questions that follow.

She dropped her glove, to prove his love, then looked at him and smiled;
He bowed, and in a moment leaped among the lions wild:

The leap was quick, return was quick, he has regained his place,
Then threw the glove, but not with love, right in the lady's face.
"By God!" said Francis, "rightly done!" and he rose from where he sat:
"No love," quoth he, "but vanity, sets love a task like that".

(i) Why did the lady smile at the Count? [Evaluative] (3)

(ii) Was her lover able to complete the task she set? [Recall] (3)

(iii) What happened at the end of the poem? [Understanding] (3)

(iv) Describe the Lady's character based on this incident. [Analysis] (3)

(v) Why did King Francis agree with the Count's actions? [Evaluative] (4)

Question 7.

Read the following extract from H.W. Longfellow's poem 'Haunted Houses' and answer the questions that follow.

We have no title-deeds to house or lands;
Owners and occupants of earlier dates
From graves forgotten stretch their dusty hands,
And hold in mortmain still their old estates.

The spirit-world around this world of sense
Floats like an atmosphere, and everywhere
Wafts through these earthly mists and vapoursdense
A vital breath of more ethereal air

(i) In the above stanza, who does 'we' refer to? [Recall] (3)

(ii) Explain the line 'from graves forgotten stretch their dusty hands'. [Understanding] (3)

(iii) What is the role of 'mists and vapours' for the 'spiritual world'? [Understanding] (3)

(iv) The poet mentions two worlds in the poem. [Recall and Understanding] (3)
What are these two worlds?
How are they connected?

SP-01

(v) What is a 'mortmain'?
What does it mean in the context of this poem? [Understanding] (4)

Answers in Topper's Style

1. (i) (b) Cassius was not as friendly as before.

(ii) (d) For being a bad poet.

(iii) (a) Brutus should never suffer the indignity of being a captive.

(iv) (b) I do know but one that unassailable holds on his rank,

(v) (a) His pragmatism

(vi) (c) Those who wish to be slaves.

(vii) (a) Photographs on the wall

(viii) (d) Impact of Death and Grief
(ix) (a) Let it lie and sleep
(x) (c) She wanted to test her love and gain everyone's attention.
(xi) (d) Alliteration
(xii) (d) None of these
(xiii) (a) He was a writer so he was creative and had individuality.
(xiv) (b) Politics Today
(xv) (c) I is the cause for II.
(xvi) (b) I, IV, III and II

2. (i) Artemidorus is feeling anxious in the above lines. This is so because he gets a letter warning him about the conspiracy against Julius Caesar. As a result, he pleads with Caesar to read the letter but to no avail.

No, his worry doesn't get resolved as he fails in warning Caesar who does not read the letter. Consequently, Caesar is later assassinated.

(ii) Artemidorus pleads with Caesar to read his letter before anything else and treat it with utmost importance.

The word 'suit' means 'meets the need of'. Artemidorus uses the word to indicate that the contents of the letter were about Caesar.

(iii) Caesar ignores Artemidorus' appeal and addresses other letters first. He declares that anything concerning him will be resolved last as the welfare of his people is of greater importance to him than his own.

Caesar's invulnerable response indicates his sense of duty and selfless nature. He took his role and responsibility earnestly. However, it also shows that he considered his private self as infallible and invulnerable to the actions of moral men.

(iv) Yes, I agree that Caesar was being stubborn. He refused to listen and understand the desperation and urgency in Artemidorus's plea. If he had paid heed to his warning, he may have not been assassinated.

(v) The given line means one's personal concerns should be one's last priority. In the context of Julius Caeser, it shows his dedication towards his country. Caesar tells Artemidorus that anything that concerns only him would be addressed at the end after the concerns of his people are sorted out. This is because he considered his people as his priority.

Yes, we can say that Caesar's decision to address the matter's concerning his people first shows a split between his public and private self. His decision demonstrates a split between his public and private self, wherein he is endangering himself by believing that his public self is so strong that his private self cannot be harmed.

3. (i) The phrase 'an itching palm' refers to accepting bribes.

Brutus uses the phrase when he learns that Cassius has been abusing his power and siphoning off money from corrupt, incompetent men. He uses the phrase for Cassius while confronting him.

(ii) Ides of March is the day of the month when Julius Caesar was murdered for his 'corrupt ways'.

Brutus reminds Cassius of the day to warn him against following Caesar's footsteps. He indicates that anyone who follows Caesar's footsteps would meet the same fate.

(iii) Cassius is offended by Brutus's allegation.

As a result, he attempts to defend himself by hiding his guilt. He threatens Brutus to watch his words and that, if he was not his friend, he would have killed Brutus on the spot.

(iv) Yes, Brutus felt that Cassius was acting like Caesar. He condemns Cassius for his dishonesty and corruption, the same things that made Brutus conspire against Caesar. He calls Cassius actions unethical and grounds for treason.

To emphasise his point, Brutus argues that he would rather be a dog than be a Roman that lacks integrity.

(v) Brutus' main argument against Cassius was the hypocrisy that Cassius displayed by siphoning money. He argues that he conspired against Caesar as he feared corruption would have plagued Rome in under Caesar's rule. However, after seeing Cassius indulge in similar practices, he calls him a hypocrite.

He doesn't take a strict action against Cassius, as he valued their brotherhood and friendship. He chooses to criticise his actions instead.

4. (i) The above line was said by the narrator to the photographer. He is feeling angry while addressing the photographer. The narrator is 40 years old.

(ii) The narrator was angry as the photographer was not pleased with the narrator's appearance. The photographer pointed out features of the narrator that he disliked and wanted to change.

Yes, he was justified in his feelings. Anyone in such a situation would have felt insulted.

(iii) The photograph was taken suddenly. The narrator was in the middle of his outburst. The photographer didn't give him any warning or wait for him to finish. He snapped the picture ubruptly during the narrator's speech.

(iv) The narrator explained that he liked the way he looked. He expressed that he was aware of his imperfections but he loved himself regardless.

The photographer didn't seem to understand the narrator's view. He shows his indifference by ignoring the narrator and clicking a picture of him while he was speaking.

(v) Yes, the narrator initially sought the photographer's approval as he is insecure about his looks. He was patient and co-operative with the photographer and tolerated all his criticism. The photographer continuously commented on his appearance but he listened patiently and complied with his instructions.

However, when he couldn't bear anymore of the photographer's indifference and insults, he snaps. He demonstrates confidence and love for his appearance. He asserts that his face may have flaws but he doesn't care and loves it as it is.

5. (i) Martin's father worked from home.

He asked Martin why he was breathless after he came home. When Martin told him he climbed the stairs, he asked him the reason for not using the elevator.

The word 'frowned' describes his confusion and frustration about Martin's response.

(ii) Martin didn't like climbing the stairs as he felt scared and uneasy. The stairwell was dark as the lights were broken and there were no windows in it. His footsteps echoed in the empty stairwell making him feel as if he was being followed.

Martin climbed sixteen floors as his home was on the seventeenth floor.

(iii) Martin perceived that his father thought him to be silly and a coward. He knew his father disapproved of him being skinny, weak and unathletic. He was upset that his own father had such a low opinion of him.

(iv) Yes, Martin decided to use the elevator the next time.

He inferred he would get accustomed to it eventually just like he became accustomed to getting bullied at school. He knew of his father's disapproval and didn't want to disappoint him more.

(v) Martin and his father didn't have a close relationship. His father didn't show affection or empathy towards Martin which made him feel lacking. His father is unsympathetic towards him and always scrutinises him for his shortcomings, like thinking he is feeble and a coward. He is harsh and unsupportive which makes Martin feel uncomfortable in sharing his fears with him.

This shows that Martin's father is a neglecting and apathetic parent. He neither takes his child's fears seriously nor does he help Martin in overcoming them.

6. (i) The lady drops her glove in the arena filled with ferocious lions to test her lover, the Count's reaction. She smiled at him to indicate the challenge she had set to him.

(ii) Yes, her lover, the Count was able to fulfill the task his lady love set for him. He bravely jumped inside the arena, picked the glove and climbed back to his place.

(iii) After the Count climbed back, he threw the glove right at his lady love's face. He does so to show his anger for her foolishness for giving him such a risky task to fulfill. He had realised that the lady threw her glove deliberately to please her vanity which for him was not an indication of love.

(iv) The lady comes across as proud, self-centered and foolish. In her hopes of gaining glory and attention from the crowd, she puts her lover in a dangerous situation without thinking about the risk and consequences of her actions.

(v) The King agreed with the Count's action because he believed that no one would put the life of their loved ones in jeopardy intentionally. If we truly love someone, we would never hurt them on purpose. Instead we would keep them away from harm as much as we can. The Lady threw her glove to gain attention and didn't think about the risk she was putting her lover in. Her actions were unjustified and self-serving.

7. (i) 'We' refers to the people who live in the house.

(ii) The given line talks about the ghosts who lived in the houses. The words 'from graves forgotten' mean that people who currently live in these houses have probably forgotten the people who lived there in the past. The memories of these ghosts have gotten lost and replaced. 'Dusty hands' is used to emphasise that these ghosts are old and go unnoticed in their 'dusty' graves.

(iii) The mists and vapours build the passage between the spiritual and the human world. They cover the Earth and act as a bridge through which spirits slip into the human dimension.

(iv) The two worlds the poet is talking about is the physical world in which we live and the spiritual world where the phantoms exist. The poet believes that both the worlds are connected by a light and 'ethereal' layer of air acting like the passage between them. He believes that these two worlds co-exist and the spirits float around the Earth like the atmosphere.

(v) The word 'mortmain' is a legal term. It is the ownership of land or buildings by a religious organisation. It is protection that makes such places 'unbuyable' even after the death of the leader of the organisation.

In the poem, the word 'mortmain' is used as a metaphor for the bond between the ghosts who owned the houses in the past and people who possess them in the present. Even though people from our past aren't with us, they continue to impact our choices and perceptions.

SQP Code : **PB-2/10** Series ***i*-Succeed 2-25/10** Roll No. | | | | | | | | |

Sample Question Paper 02

Literature in English 10th (Code 01)

Time : 2 Hrs.

Max. Marks : 80

General Instructions

1. You will not be allowed to write during the first 15 minutes. This time is to be spent in reading the question paper.
2. The time given at the head of this paper is the time allowed for writing the answers.
3. The paper has four Sections.
4. Section A is compulsory - All questions in Section A must be answered.
5. You must attempt one question from each of the Sections B, C and D and one other question from any section of your choice.
6. The intended marks for questions or parts of questions are given in brackets [ ].

ection A (Attempt all questions from this Section)

uestion 1.

oose the correct answer to the questions from the given options. (16)

(i) Cassius thought he was superior to Brutus because he was .... and .... [Recall]

(a) a brave soldier, could manage conflicts better
(b) a brave soldier, could remain calm during conflicts better
(c) a more experienced soldier, could remain calm during conflicts better
(d) a more experienced soldier, could manage conflicts better

(ii) At the battle of Philippi, what blame does Titinius place on Brutus? [Understanding]

(a) Brutus allowed premature attack.
(b) Brutus's troops ran away like cowards.
(c) Brutus's troops allowed Antony to surround them.
(d) Brutus didn't allow the men to retreat from the battle.

(iii) .... is the first person to stab Caesar. [Recall]

(a) Brutus (b) Casca
(c) Cinna (d) Decius

(iv) Antony said that he wouldn't wrong the 'honourable men'. Who would he rather wrong? [Understanding]

(a) Caesar (b) The people of France
(c) His masters (d) The dead and himself

(v) 'If it were so, it was a grievous fault;

And grievously hath Caesar answer'd it.'

What does 'grievous fault' mean in the above lines? [Understanding]

(a) Caesar's anger
(b) Caesar's love for Rome
(c) Caesar's over-ambition
(d) Caesar's dedication

(vi) What did Brutus get to know about Cassius army? [Recall]

(a) Cassius army will return to Sardis with regards and honour.
(b) Cassius main cavalry will arrive at Sardis with Cassius.
(c) Cassius army is unwilling to camp at Sardis.
(d) Cassius army will arrive at Sardis before Cassius to set up camp.

(vii) What is the figure of speech used in the line 'We breathe, briefly' from the poem 'When Great Trees Fall'? [Understanding]

(a) Simile
(b) Metaphor
(c) Imagery
(d) Alliteration

(viii) In the poem 'Haunted houses', the poet possessed the power .... [Analysis]

(a) to capture ghosts
(b) to do exorcism
(c) to communicate with ghosts
(d) to see the ghosts

(ix) In the poem 'The Glove and the Lions', what was the King's nature? [Recall]

(a) Cheerful
(b) Boastful
(c) Sincere
(d) Proud

(x) Select the option that shows the correct relationship between Statements (I) and (II) from Robert Frost's poem 'A Considerable Speck'. [Analysis]

Statement I The poem is about the importance of using one's mind.

Statement II The poem criticises dull people who don't use their minds productively.

(a) I is true and II is false.
(b) II is true and I is false.
(c) I and II are both true.
(d) I and II are both false.

(xi) How did the animals react to Bhisma's singing in the poem 'The Power of Music'? [Understanding]

SP-02

(a) They run away.
(b) They dance to his singing.
(c) They fall asleep listening to it.
(d) None of these

(xii) In Ama Ata Aidoo's short story 'The Girl Who Can', what is the only acceptable reason for Nana for not having 'good legs'? [Recall]

(a) The girl didn't have limbs.
(b) The girl was mentally challenged.
(c) The girl was a teenager.
(d) The girl was unmarried.

(xiii) Choose the option that lists the sequence of events from Ray Bradbury's short story 'The Pedestrian' in the correct order. [Recall]

I. The police car warned Mr. Mead to stand back.
II. As expected by Mr. Mead, the police car had no police man inside it.
III. Mr. Mead was out for a walk.
IV. Mr. Mead told the police that he was a writer.

(a) I, III, II and IV
(b) I, IV, III and II
(c) III, II, I and IV
(d) III, I, IV and II

(xiv) In the short story 'With the Photographer', the narrator thinks that the photographer was going to kiss him because .... [Recall]

(a) the photographer was leaning closely towards him
(b) the photographer closed his eyes
(c) the photographer grabbed his head and twisted it to the side
(d) the photographer was staring at him suggestively

(xv) What did M. Hamel buy on the last day of school in the short story 'The Last Lesson'? [Recall]

(a) A camera
(b) A French book
(c) A box of sweets
(d) A stack of new copies

(xvi) What animal does Martin compare the fat lady to in the short story 'The Elevator'? [Recall]

(a) Elephant
(b) Walrus
(c) Pig
(d) Alligator

Section B (Answer one or more questions from this Section)

DRAMA

Julius Caesar

By William Shakespeare

Question 2.

Read the extract given below and answer the questions that follow.

"A curse shall light upon the limbs of men;
Domestic fury and fierce civil strife
Shall cumber all the parts of Italy;
Blood and destruction shall be so in use
And dreadful objects so familiar
That mothers shall but smile when they behold
Their infants quarter'd with the hands of war;
All pity choked with custom of fell deeds:
And Caesar's spirit, ranging for revenge,
With Ate by his side come hot from hell,"

(i) Who is the speaker of the above lines?
Where is he/she while giving this speech?
Explain what emotions they are feeling in brief. [Recall and Understanding] (3)

(ii) How does the speaker express their grief?
What is the meaning of 'fierce civil strife'? [Recall and Understanding] (3)

(iii) Explain the meaning of the line "All pity choked with custom of fell deeds". [Analysis] (3)

(iv) Who was 'Ate'?
Why is he/she mentioned in the speaker's monologue? [Recall and Understanding] (3)

(v) The speaker forecasts that Rome is on the road to destruction.
Why do they think so?
What do they think will happen? [Evaluative] (4)

SP-02

Question 3.

Read the extract given below and answer the questions that follow.

Cassius : "Come down, behold no more.
O, coward that I am, to live so long,
To see my best friend ta'en before my face!
[Pindarus descends]
Come hither, sirrah:
In Parthia did I take thee prisoner;
And then I swore thee, saving of thy life,
That whatsoever I did bid thee do,
Thou shouldst attempt it. Come now, keep thine oath;
Now be a freeman : and with this good sword,
That ran through Caesar's bowels, search this bosom.
Stand not to answer: here, take thou the hilts;
And, when my face is cover'd, as 'tis now,
Guide thou the sword.
[Pindarus stabs Cassius.]
Caesar, thou art revenged,
Even with the sword that kill'd thee."

(i) What does Cassius hear about his friend, Titinius?
How does he react? **[Recall and understanding] (3)**

(ii) Why does Cassius call himself a coward?
Which line in the extract suggests this? **[Recall and understanding] (3)**

(iii) What does Cassius ask Pindarus to do in the above extract?
Does Pindarus grant his wish? **[Recall and understanding] (3)**

(iv) Where did Cassius meet Pindarus?
How did Cassius help him?
What did Cassius ask for in return? **[Recall and understanding] (3)**

(v) Explain 'with the sword that kill'd thee'.
Do you think Cassius is regretful of killing Caesar? Why? **[Evaluative and Analysis] (4)**

Section C (Answer one or more questions from this Section)

PROSE-SHORT STORIES

(Treasure Chest - A Collection of ICSE Short Stories and Poems)

Question 4.

Read the following extract from Ama Ata Aidoo's short story 'The Girl Who Can' and answer the questions that follow.

And Nana would shake her head.
Maami: 'Mother, why are you always complaining about Adjoa's legs? If you ask me....'

Nana: 'They are too thin. And I am not asking you' !

Nana has many voices. There is a special one she uses to shut everyone up.

'Some people have no legs at all,' my mother would try again with all her small courage.

'But Adjoa has legs,' Nana would insist; 'except that they are too thin. And also too long for a woman. Kaya, listen. Once in a while, but only once in a very long while, somebody decides - nature, a child's spirit mother, an accident happens, and somebody gets born without arms, or legs, or both sets of limbs. And then let me touch wood: it is a sad business. And you know, such things are not for talking about everyday. But if any female child decides to come into this world with legs, then they might as well be legs.'

(i) Whose legs are too thin?
Who thinks that?
Does Kaya think the same? [Recall and understanding] (3)

(ii) Who are the two important people in Adjoa's life?
Do they have the same opinion about her upbringing? [Recall and understanding] (3)

(iii) According to Nana, what is the importance of strong legs? [Recall] (3)

(iv) What is Nana's opinion about school?
Does Maami agree with her opinion? [Recall and understanding] (3)

(v) What is the relationship dynamic between Nana and Maami?
Mention sentences from the above extract that depict their personalities. [Recall and understanding] (4)

Question 5.

Read the following extract from Stephen Leacock's short story 'With the Photographer' and answer the questions that follow.

"Oh, no," he answered, "I've retouched them. They come out splendidly, don't they?"

"Fine," I said, "but surely my eyebrows are not like that?"

"No," said the photographer, with a momentary glance at my face, "the eyebrows are removed. We have a process now-the Delphide-for putting in new ones. You'll notice here where we've applied it to carry the hair away from the brow. I don't like the hair low on the skull."

(i) What does 'them' refer to in the first line?
Why were they retouched?
What did the photographer feel about his edit? [Recall and understanding] (3)

(ii) Were any other features retouched by the photographer?
If yes, list the ones mentioned in the above extract. [Recall] (3)

(iii) What method did the photographer use to edit the pictures? [Understanding] (3)

(iv) How did the narrator feel about the edits?
If you were in his place, would you feel the same? [Understanding] (3)

(v) Why did the photographer not like the narrator's eyebrows?
Did he plan to make any more changes to the photo? How? [Understanding and Analysis] (4)

Section D (Answer one or more questions from this Section)

POETRY

(Treasure Chest - A Collection of ICSE SHort Stories and Poems)

Question 6.

Read the following extract from H. W. Longfellow's poem 'Haunted Houses' and answer the questions that follow.

"There are more guests at table than the hosts
Invited; the illuminated hall
Is thronged with quiet, inoffensive ghosts,
As silent as the pictures on the wall.
The stranger at my fireside cannot see
The forms I see, nor hear the sounds i hear;
He but perceives what is; while unto me
All that has been is visible and clear."

(i) What does the speaker find unusual? [Recall] (3)

(ii) What is the behaviour of the ghosts in the halls? [Recall] (3)

(iii) Which line in the above extract uses simile? Explain the line. [Understanding] (3)

(iv) Explain how the speaker is different from the stranger by the fireside. [Analysis] (3)

(v) What is the theme of the poem 'Haunted Houses'? [Understanding] (4)

Question 7.

Read the following extract from Maya Angelou's poem 'When Great Trees Fall' and answer the questions that follow.

"When great souls die,
the air around us becomes
light, rare, sterile.
We breathe briefly.
Our eyes, briefly,
see with
a hurtful clarity.
Our memory, suddenly sharpened,
examines,
gnaws on kind words
unsaid,
promised walks
never taken".

(i) Who are 'great souls'? [Recall] (3)

(ii) What happens when great souls die? [Recall] (3)

(iii) What do we see with 'hurtful clarity'? [Understanding] (3)

(iv) What happens to the air around us after great souls die? What words did the poet use to describe it? [Understanding] (3)

(v) Explain the line— 'Our memory, suddenly sharpened, examines, gnaws on kind words unsaid'. [Analysis] (4)

Answers in Topper's Style

1. (i) (d) a more experienced soldier, could manage conflicts better.
   (ii) (a) Brutus allowed premature attack.
   (iii) (b) Casca
   (iv) (d) The dead and himself
   (v) (c) Caesar's over-ambition
   (vi) (b) Cassius's main cavalry will arrive at Sardis with Cassius.
   (vii) (d) Alliteration
   (viii) (d) To see the ghosts
   (ix) (a) Cheerful
   (x) (c) I and II are both true.
   (xi) (a) They run away.
   (xii) (a) The girl didn't have limbs.
   (xiii) (d) III, I, IV, II
   (xiv) (c) the photographer grabbed his head and twisted it to the side
   (xv) (d) A stack of new copies
   (xvi) (c) Pig

2. (i) Antony is the speaker of the given lines.

   He is alone with Caesar's corpse, at the senate.

   He is overwhelmed by grief and anger. He struggles to understand the senator's deceit and predicts that Rome will soon fall as a consequence of betraying Caesar.

   (ii) Antony is upset seeing his friend lying in a pool of blood. He expresses his anger at seeing a great ruler come to a brutal end and is filled with resentment for being gentle with the conspirators.

   "Fierce civil strife" means "aggressive conflict between two organisations/groups of the same country". Antony predicts that Caesar's death will lead to civil conflicts within Italy.

   (iii) Antony believes that Caesar's assassination will lead Rome to the path of anarchy and bloodshed. If that happens, a civil war will break out and crime rates will peak. This will further lead to 'choking' or obstruction of feelings like compassion and pity among the people of Rome.

   (iv) 'Ate' is the Greek goddess of revenge and mischief.

   Ate was banished from Olympus for provoking Gods and man to irrational acts of violence. Antony thinks Caesar's assassination was unjust. He presumes that Caesar's demise will lead Italy to the road of destruction.
   He also presumes that soon Caesar's spirit will extract revenge on his conspirators with Ate beside him.

   (v) As Caesar was a great leader, Antony anticipates Rome will fall after Caesar's death. He predicts bloodshed and decay of morals. Human emotions like compassion and humanity will erode human senses. He predicts that violence will become common so much so that mothers will become accustomed to the sight of their children being slaughtered.

   Rome will become home to anarchy wherein unjust violence and death would become a norm.

3. (i) Cassius hears that Titinius was captured by the enemy forces.

   He is heartbroken to learn of his friend's capture and breaks down in despair.

   (ii) Cassius considered himself a coward because he watched his best friend get captured while he stood there doing nothing. He cannot bear his failure.

   The lines 'O, coward that I am, to live so long, To see my best friend ta'en before my face!' suggest the same.

   (iii) Cassius asks Pindarus to kill him with his sword by thrusting it into his chest. He forbids him to ask any questions and ask him to kill him the moment he covers his head.

   Yes, Pindarus grants his wish with a heavy heart.

   (iv) Cassius met Pindarus in Parthia where Pindarus was a prisoner of war.

   Cassius helped him by sparing his life. However, he didn't do it for free. He made Pindarus swear to grant him a favour back whenever Cassius demanded it and to do so without asking any question.

(v) The given statement indicates that the sword which had been used to kill Julius Caesar will now kill those murderers. Cassius wants to be killed by the same sword by which he had killed Caesar. In this manner, the sword would have avenged Caesar's death.

I do not think that Cassius is regretful of killing Caesar. Cassius is regretful of losing Titinius in the battle and, thus, had lost all hope. This is why he wants to die and not because of his regret for murdering Caesar.

4. (i) Nana thinks that Adjoa's legs are too thin.

Kaya, Adjoa's mother, disagrees with Nana.

(ii) Nana and Maami (Kaya) are Adjoa's family. They disagree on many aspects of Adjoa's upbringing.

(iii) Nana associates strong legs with a woman's childbearing capabilities. She believes that a woman's principal duty is to carry and give birth to healthy children. She argues that only a woman with strong hips and legs can bear healthy children.

(iv) Nana doesn't approve of sending Adjoa to school. She doesn't see the merit in educating her as she expects her to marry and manage a household.

Maami supports Adjoa's education. She recognises the importance and benefits of schooling. She wishes Adjoa to live in a different and more independent future.

(v) Nana and Maami have a disbalanced dynamic in terms of power and authority which is in Nana's favour. They love each other like any mother-daughter duo. However, Nana is assertive, authoritative and orthodox. She speaks her mind and expects respect and obedience from Maami and Adjoa in most situations. Maami, on the other hand, is soft and timid. Her repentance for her past mistakes leads her to submit to her mother's wishes and taunts.

Sentence that depicts Nana's personality: 'They are too thin. And I am not asking you'!

Sentence that depicts Maami's personality: 'Some people have no legs at all,' my mother would try again with all her small courage.

5. (i) 'Them' refers to the narrator's eyes in the first line.

The photographer retouched the narrator's eyes in the photo as the original didn't flatter him.

He was pleased with his edit and remarked that they came out 'splendidly'.

(ii) Yes, the photographer retouched other features of the narrator.

The above extract mentions his eyebrows as one of the edited features.

(iii) The photographer used the new technique of Delphide to edit the pictures.

(iv) The narrator left disheartened and frustrated about the edits. The photographer's insensitivity towards his appearance leaves him shattered in tears. His insecurities are awoken and he feels humiliated by the photographer's ignorance towards his feelings.

If I were in his place, I would have felt the same.

(v) The photographer didn't like the narrator's eyebrows as he didn't have an ideal brow line with excess hair. He critiqued the hair low on the narrator's skull and removed it using the Delphide method. He planned to edit the narrator's ears. He planned to remove them completely using the new Sulphide technique.

6. (i) The speaker finds the guests to be unusual as he realises that the dinner table holds more people than invited. The ghosts who lived in the house in the past co-exist with the people who live there now.

(ii) The ghosts are quiet and harmless. They are not offended, evil souls and pose no threat to the people living in the house.

(iii) The line "As silent as the pictures on the wall." contains a simile. The line presents the nature of the ghosts in the houses. The quiet and harmless ghosts are compared to pictures that hang on the walls of the corridor. These pictures are silent and, offer no interference in any living being's life like the ghosts that exist in these houses.

(iv) The speaker differs from the stranger by the fireside for their extraordinary ability. The stranger can feel the ghosts' presence but the speaker claims to possess the power to see and hear the ghosts that wander the houses clearly.

(v) The theme of the poem 'Haunted Houses' is that houses hold memories and phantoms of the people who had once lived in it. He emphasises on the transient nature of time and human existence. He argues that material possession will deteriorate but people move on through their memories.

Memories hold immense power and memories from our loved ones can impact our lives even after they are gone.

7. (i) 'Great souls' are prominent people in our lives. These people can be a wise relative you respect or a popular figure you consider as your role model.

(ii) The death of a great soul is a massive loss. When a prominent soul dies, people feel suffocated by the intensity of their grief. The air around them feels flimsy and thin. Isolation plagues their lives and their body feels empty. Any memory of them brings back the pain of losing them. Any regret or unsaid words haunt their dreams.

(iii) We see the memories we made with our loved ones with 'hurtful clarity'. After they depart, their memories make us nostalgic and remind us of all the moments we spend together. But these memories are now bittersweet in their absence as they are also a painful reminder of their demise.

(iv) In the absence of the great soul, the air around us becomes so thin and flimsy that it hinders our breathing, suffocating us with the heaviness of grief. The poet used the words 'light', 'rare' and 'sterile' to describe it. The words 'light' and 'rare' are used to emphasise the scarcity of air surrounding us. 'Sterile' denotes the lack of creativity in our life.

(v) Memories hold a lot of power. They are capable of evoking strong emotions in oneself. Once we lose a pivotal member of our life, their memories can provide us with strength to move on. But when our loss is new, our memories are fresh and strong. Questions of 'what ifs' or 'if onlys' fill our thoughts unexpectedly, inflicting pain like a sharp tool that suddenly gnaws on our skin. We regret 'kind words' that we never spoke before but wanted to.

SQP Code : **PB-3/10** | Series *i*-**Succeed 3-25/10** | Roll No. | | | | | | | |

Sample Question Paper 03

Literature in English 10th (Code 01)

General Instructions

1. You will not be allowed to write during the first 15 minutes. This time is to be spent in reading the question paper.
2. The time given at the head of this paper is the time allowed for writing the answers.
3. The paper has four Sections.
4. Section A is compulsory - All questions in Section A must be answered.
5. You must attempt one question from each of the Sections B, C and D and one other question from any section of your choice.
6. The intended marks for questions or parts of questions are given in brackets [ ].

Time : 2 Hrs.

Max. Marks : 80

Section A (Attempt all questions from this Section)

Question 1.

Choose the correct answer to the questions from the given options. (16)

(i) Cassius refers to himself as a 'coward' after Titinius is taken captive. Why? [Understanding]

(a) He was hiding while his men were getting slaughtered in the battlefield.
(b) He had lived long enough to see his friend be taken captive.
(c) He allowed Brutus to run the battle strategy.
(d) He asks Pindarus to kill him so no one else can.

(ii) 'Blood and destruction shall be so in use
And dreadful objects so familiar
That mothers shall but smile when they behold
Their infants quarter'd with the hands of war;
All pity choked with custom of fell deeds:'

What does the phrase 'All pity choked' mean here? [Understanding]

(a) People will have no pity. (b) People will become sympathetic.
(c) People will become choked. (d) People will have no anger.

(iii) Brutus condemns Cassius for siphoning off money. He asks Cassius to use the gold to .... [Recall]

(a) pay his soldiers (b) buy food and supplies for the army
(c) buy gifts for his friends (d) return it back to the bribers

(iv) Caesar thought he was as constant as .... [Recall]

(iv) Caesar thought he was as constant as .... [Recall]

(a) Rome
(b) the Southern cross
(c) Mount Olympus
(d) the Northern star

(v) In Act IV Scene 3, what information does Messala deliver to Brutus and Cassius? [Recall]

(a) Antony and Octavius are planning to attack Philippi.
(b) Antony is planning to execute Octavius.
(c) Antony is the new emperor.
(d) Octavius is planning to attack Philippi.

(vi) What does Antony claim lives on after men? [Recall]

(a) Their ambitions
(b) Their wealth
(c) Their evil deeds
(d) Their good deeds

(vii) In Robert Frost's poem 'A Considerable Speck', the mite paused because .... [Analysis]

(a) it was attracted to the ink on the paper
(b) it was suspicious of the writer
(c) it had an obstacle in his way
(d) it needed to think about its next steps

(viii) The Lady dropped her glove in the arena .... [Recall]

(a) to distract the Count
(b) to test her lover
(c) to gain the King's love
(d) to be friend the lions

(ix) Who rescues everyone from Bhisma's bad singing in 'The Power of Music ? [Recall]

(a) Cow
(b) Horse
(c) Goat
(d) Turtle

(x) When great souls die, the air around us becomes light, rare, ...

Complete the given line from the poem 'When Great trees fall'. [Recall]

(a) sterile
(b) empty
(c) soothing
(d) electric

(xi) Select the option that shows the correct relationship between Statements (I) and (II) from H. W. Longfellow's poem 'Haunted Houses'. [Analysis]

Statement I The souls who depart from Earth still linger in their former living spaces.

Statement II The ghosts seek claim on their former living spaces by haunting them.

(a) I is true and II is false.
(b) II is true and I is false.
(c) I is the cause for II.
(d) I and II are independent of each other.

(xii) In 'The Elevator', Martin felt like he was being chased on the stairs because .... [Understanding]

(a) the stairs were cold
(b) his footsteps echoed against the cement
(c) the stairs had dark shadows
(d) he kept hearing eerie voices behind him

(xiii) In Alphonse Daudet's short story 'The Last Lesson', M. Hamel complains that the parents preferred to send their kids to .... instead of school in the past. [Recall]

(a) church
(b) farms and mills
(c) relative's house
(d) work at the factory

(xiv) By the end of the short story 'The Girl Who Can', what does Nana realise? [Understanding]

(a) Her granddaughter was a great runner. (b) Her daughter should get an education.
(c) Legs can have many uses. (d) Her granddaughter is ready for marriage.

(xv) In the short story 'The Pedestrian', where is Mr. Mead taken to in the end? [Recall]

(a) The police station (b) The psychiatric facility
(c) The library (d) The homeless shelter

(xvi) Choose the option that lists the sequence of events from Stephen Leacock's short story 'With the photographer' in the correct order. [Recall]

I. The photographer rolled the camera into the room.
II. The photographer put a black cloth over himself.
III. The photographer tore at the cotton sheet with a hooked stick.
IV. The photographer went behind the camera again.

(a) I, III, II and IV (b) I, III, IV and II (c) I, II, III and IV (d) I, IV, II and III

Section B (Answer one or more questions from this Section)

DRAMA

Julius Caesar

By William Shakespeare

Question 2.

Read the extract given below and answer the questions that follow.

"Thou hast described
A hot friend cooling: ever note, Lucilius,
When love begins to sicken and decay,
It useth an enforced ceremony.
There are no tricks in plain and simple faith;
But hollow men, like horses hot at hand,
Make gallant show and promise of their mettle;
But when they should endure the bloody spur,
They fall their crests, and like deceitful jades,
Sink in the trial. Comes his army on" ?

SP-03

(i) Are these lines spoken by Brutus?
Who is he speaking to (listener)?
Who are they talking about (subject of their conversation)? [Recall and Understanding] (3)

(ii) What is the meaning of the phrase 'A hot friend cooling'?
Why did the speaker say this? [Recall and Understanding] (3)

(iii) What is the meaning of "horse hot at hand"?
What are such 'horses' compared to? [Recall and Understanding] (3)

(iv) 'Comes his army on?' Who is 'his' in this sentence?
Where do they plan on approaching? [Recall and Understanding] (3)

(v) In Act IV Scene 2, what is the cause of the tense environment in Brutus' tent?
What does Brutus suggest to resolve it? [Recall and Analysis] (4)

Question 3.

Read the extract given below and answer the questions that follow.

"Gentlemen all, - alas! What shall I say?
My credit now stands on such slippery ground,
That one of two bad ways you must conceit me,
Either a coward or a flatterer.
That I did love thee, Caesar, O'tis true:
If then thy spirit look upon us now,
Shall it not grieve thee dearer than thy death,"

(i) Who is the speaker of the above lines?
Who are the 'Gentlemen' he/she is addressing to? [Recall and Understanding] (3)

(ii) What sight does the speaker claim will make Caesar grieve dearer than death?
To whom does the speaker compare Caesar and the 'Gentlemen' to later in this scene? [Recall and Understanding] (3)

(iii) Later in this scene, the speaker requests Brutus for two things. What are they?
What are Brutus conditions for fulfilling the requests? [Recall and Understanding] (3)

(iv) Explain the meaning of the line 'My credit now stands on such slippery ground'.
What does the speaker think the 'Gentlemen' will perceive him as?
Which line expresses the speaker's love for Caesar? [Analysis and Understanding] (3)

(v) Antony is a true friend and a skilled commander.
Do you agree with the above statement? Justify. [Evaluative] (4)

Section C (Answer one or more questions from this Section)

PROSE-SHORT STORIES

(Treasure Chest - A Collection of ICSE Short Stories and Poems)

SP-03

Question 4.

Read the following extract from William Sleator's short story 'The Elevator' and answer the questions that follow.

"Now she knows I live on the seventeen," he thought.
"Have you ever noticed a strange lady in the elevator?" he asked his father that evening.
"Can't say I have," he replied, not looking away from the television.
Martin knew he was probably making a mistake, but he had to tell somebody about the woman, "She was in the elevator with me twice today. She just kept staring at me. She never stopped looking at me for a minute".

(i) What floor did Martin live on?
Who is he referring to as 'she' in the first line?
Why does he not want her to know where he lived? [Recall and Understanding] (3)

(ii) What did Martin ask his father that evening?
What did his father reply? [Recall] (3)

(iii) How did Martin feel about the fat lady? [Understanding] (3)

(iv) What mistake did Martin think he was making?

Was he correct? [Recall and Understanding] (3)

(v) Did Martin get any help from his father? Why or why not? [Analysis] (4)

Question 5.

Read the following extract from Ray Bradbury's short story 'The Pedestrian' and answer the questions that follow.

The car hesitated, or rather gave a faint whirring click, as if information, somewhere, was dropping card by punch-slotted card under electric eyes. 'To the Psychiatric Center for Research on Regressive Tendencies.'

He got in. The door shut with a soft thud.

The police car rolled through the night avenues, flashing its dim lights ahead.

They passed one house on one street a moment later, one house in an entire city of houses that were dark, but this one particular house had all its electric lights brightly lit, every window a loud yellow illumination, square and warm in the cool darkness.

(i) What stops Mr. Mead on the streets?

What is he asked to do?

Describe how it looked from inside. [Recall and Understanding] (3)

(ii) Where is the car taking Mr. Mead?

Why? [Understanding and Analysis] (3)

(iii) According to you, how is Mr. Mead feeling about his situation? [Understanding] (3)

(iv) What did they pass on their way to the facility?

Why does it stand out from its surroundings? [Recall and Understanding] (3)

(v) What is Mr. Mead's profession?

Does he have a family?

What could have saved Mr. Mead from his fate? [Recall and Understanding] (4)

SP-03

Section D (Answer one or more questions from this Section)

POETRY

(Treasure Chest - A Collection of ICSE Short Stories and Poems)

Question 6.

Read the following extract from Leigh Hunt's poem 'The Glove and the Lions' and answer the questions that follow.

"De Lorge's love o'erheard the King, a beauteous lively dame
With smiling lips and sharp bright eyes, which always seemed the same;
She thought, the Count my lover is brave as brave can be;
He surely would do wondrous things to show his love of me;
King, ladies, lovers, all look on; the occasion is divine;
I'll drop my glove, to prove his love; great glory will be mine".

(i) Describe the Count's lady love. [Understanding] (3)

(ii) What did the lady think about the Count? [Recall] (3)

(iii) What did the lady hear the King say? [Recall] (3)

(iv) What does the lady plan to do in the above text? [Understanding] (3)

(v) List the reason behind the lady's plan. [Evaluative] (4)

Question 7.

Read the following extract from Robert Frost's poem 'A Considerable Speck' and answer the questions that follow.

"It faltered: I could see it hesitate;
Then in the middle of the open sheet
Cower down in desperation to accept
Whatever I accorded it of fate.
I have none of the tenderer-than-thou
Collectivistic regimenting love
With which the modern world is being swept".

(i) Why did the mite hesitate? [Understanding] (3)

(ii) Explain the line "Collectivistic regimenting love". [Analysis] (3)

(iii) What did the mite do after it reached the middle of the page? [Recall] (3)

(iv) Do you think the mite made the correct decision?
Do you think it had a choice? Why? [Recall and Understanding] (3)

(v) What is the truth of the modern world according to the poet?
What flaws does he find in the mindset of people? [Recall](4)

Answers in Topper's Style

1. (i) (b) He had lived long enough to see his friend be taken captive.
   (ii) (a) People will have no pity.
   (iii) (a) pay his soldiers
   (iv) (d) the Northern star
   (v) (a) Antony and Octavius are planning to attack Philippi.
   (vi) (c) Their evil deeds
   (vii) (d) It needed to think about its next steps
   (viii) (b) To test her lover
   (ix) (c) Goat
   (x) (a) Sterile
   (xi) (a) I is true and II is false.
   (xii) (b) His footsteps echoed against the cement
   (xiii) (b) Farms and mills
   (xiv) (c) Legs can have many uses
   (xv) (b) The psychiatric facility
   (xvi) (b) I, III, IV and II

2. (i) Yes, the above lines were spoken by Brutus.

   He was speaking to Lucilius.

   They were discussing the recent changes in Cassius behaviour towards them.

   (ii) Brutus used the phrase 'A hot friend cooling' for Cassius. He believed that his friendship with Cassius had 'cooled off' or, in other words, dulled out.

   Lucilius shared with Brutus that Cassius treated him with respect but was overly formal. He appeared cold and withdrawn unlike the brotherhood he had felt before. This made Brutus call Cassius's conduct as cold and strained.

   (iii) 'Horse hot at hand' refers to horses that appear strong and ready for use.

   Brutus compares horses with hollow and insincere men. He remarks that shallow men are often boastful about their valor and merit but, in reality, they are fragile and get cold feet under pressure.

   (iv) Cassius is referred to as 'his' in the sentence.

   Brutus is inquiring about Cassius whereabouts from Lucilius. He informs Brutus that Cassius is planning to reach Sardis with his cavalry soon.

   (v) The environment inside Brutus' tent is tense because of the dynamic between Brutus and Cassius. Who feels disrespected by Brutus leading to him acting cold towards the latter.

   Brutus suggests resolving their issues inside the tent, away from the troops. He understands the importance of unity and the role it plays in boosting a soldier's morale. He asks Cassius to address all their disagreements to rebuild trust among themselves which will be essential for the upcoming war.

3. (i) Antony is the speaker of the above lines.

   He is addressing the group of people who conspired against Caesar as 'Gentlemen'.

   (ii) Antony was a close friend of Caesar. He claims that the sight of him shaking hands in peace with Caesar's assassinators while Caesar's corpse is beside them will make Caesar grieve greater than death.

   Antony compares Caesar to a brave deer. As the 'Gentlemen' are the group of conspirators, Antony compares them to hounds. He chooses this analogy as just like the hounds, the conspirators had hunted Caesar down and killed him, like a deer.

   (iii) Antony requests Brutus to allow him to display Caesar's corpse at the market place and deliver a speech at his funeral as his friend.

   Brutus grants his wish but puts forward conditions of his own. He instructs Antony to address the crowd after him. He demands that Antony acknowledge the permission Brutus and Cassius gave him publicly and not blame the conspirators for Caesar's demise. He, however, promises to allow Antony to praise Caesar to a limit.

   (iv) Antony expresses that his reputation and dignity is in danger of being unreliable. He is torn between his grief for his friend's murder and his acceptance of his friend's killers.

   Antony believes that his reputation is at risk and the 'Gentlemen' might perceive him as either a coward or a groveller.

   The line 'That I did love thee, Caesar, O'tis true:' expresses Antony's love for Caesar.

   (v) Yes, I agree with the given statement. Antony's love for Caesar was unmatched. He tricked Brutus into believing his compliance and asked for permission to speak at Caesar's funeral, he used the opportunity to drive the crowd against the conspirators. He led his and Octavius's troops and won the war against the more experienced Cassius. He avenged his friend's murder and proved himself as a true friend and a skilled military commander.

4. (i) Martin lived on the seventeenth floor.

He is referring to the creepy fat lady in the elevator as 'she' in the first line.

Martin found his experience with the fat lady frightening. He feared another encounter with her and didn't want her to have any knowledge about her.

(ii) Martin enquired if his father knew who the strange lady was.

His father was distracted by the television but admitted to not know her.

(iii) Martin felt uneasy around the fat lady. He feels intimidated by her continuous staring and large size. He feels suffocated when he travels in the elevator with her.

(iv) Martin didn't have a strong relationship with his father as the latter criticises him for his cowardice. He believes sharing his concerns about the fat lady with his father is a mistake. He fears giving his father another reason to think less of him.

Yes, he is correct in his deduction as his father doesn't take his concerns seriously.

(v) No, Martin's father was no help. He was dismissive and unsympathetic of Martin's concerns and fears. His perception of Martin is that of a weak and timid boy. As he had never seen the fat lady before, he didn't believe Martin's words. He also fails to see why her presence is of alarm to Martin, and believes he is just over-reacting.

5. (i) A police car stops Mr. Mead on the streets.

Mr. Mead is asked to stop initially by the police. Later, they ask him to sit inside the car.

The back seat of the car had bars making it look like a prison cell.

(ii) The car is taking Mr. Mead to the Psychiatric Center for Research on Regressive Tendencies.

The police car found Mr. Mead roaming around the empty streets at an unusual time. This raised an alarm for the police as all people in the city were expected to watch television at home at that time of the day. Finding Mr. Mead in the streets was unusual and unheard of.

(iii) Mr. Mead feels powerless about his situation. He is aware of his innocence but is unable to reason with the robot controlling the police car.

(iv) They passed Mr. Mead's house on their way.

His house stands out for being the only house illuminated with electric lights.

(v) Mr. Mead is a writer however he has not written anything in years.

The story doesn't say if Mr. Mead has a family.

The police car informs Mr. Mead that he could have avoided his visit to the psychiatric facility if he had a wife or a partner to provide an alibi for his whereabouts.

6. (i) Count's lady love is a beautiful lady. She is described as a lively looking girl. She has distinct, bright eyes with a smile on her lips.

(ii) The lady believed in the Count's valor. She was aware of his capabilities and chivalrous nature.

(iii) The lady heard the King talk about his privilege and that of his subjects. He jokes about how he and his subjects are lucky to be sitting outside the arena, away from the ferocious lions.

(iv) The lady plans to test the Count's love for her. She decides to drop her glove in the arena full of the dangerous lions and see his reaction.

(v) The lady wanted to acquire attention and glory from the audience and the King. She was aware of the Count's courage and deduced that his honour would make him retrieve her glove. She wanted the Count to succeed in retrieving her glove from the 'grasps' of the dangerous lions. She believed that this would establish her superiority among her peers and she would become the object of everyone's envy.

7. (i) The Mite was scared of the poet and the vastness of the white paper. It hesitated as it was not sure if it would cross the paper alive.

(ii) "Collectivistic regimenting love" means collectivistic people's control for love. This line is used to paint the irony of the modern world. People that believe in collectivism or collective control over things, like love, consider themselves superior. They act high and above everything but, in actuality, conspire to destroy anyone they consider inferior regardless of their wisdom or merit.

(iii) The mite crouched down in fear of the poet, ready to accept its fate that the poet had decided for it.

(iv) Yes, the mite made the correct decision.

It didn't have a choice.

The poet was significantly larger and faster than the mite. Like the underprivileged people in the society, the mite didn't contain the power. They are at the mercy of the rich people that have the means to rewrite their history.

(v) The poet complains about the modern world's inclination towards Collectivism.

Collectivistic individuals do not value the creativity the weaker groups have to offer. They mindlessly try to dominate or destroy weaker groups, to establish their superiority. The poet criticises such people. He believes in the strength of Individualism. He emphasises that a poor individual with their own beliefs and thoughts is far more valuable than a rich individual with no pursuits of their own.

SQP Code : **PB-4/10** | Series ***i*-Succeed 4-25/10** | Roll No.

Sample Question Paper 04

Literature in English 10th (Code 01)

General Instructions

1. You will not be allowed to write during the first 15 minutes. This time is to be spent in reading the question paper.
2. The time given at the head of this paper is the time allowed for writing the answers.
3. The paper has four Sections.
4. Section A is compulsory - All questions in Section A must be answered.
5. You must attempt one question from each of the Sections B, C and D and one other question from any section of your choice.
6. The intended marks for questions or parts of questions are given in brackets [ ].

Time : 2 Hrs.

Max. Marks : 80

Section A (Attempt all questions from this Section)

Question 1.

Choose the correct answer to the question from the given options. (16)

(i) Why is Cassius angry with Brutus? [Understanding]

(a) For questioning Cassius's military experience.
(b) For showing favouritism towards Lucilius.
(c) For not defending Pella.
(d) For calling Cassius out for bribery.

(ii) Why does Antony want to address the crowd at Caesar's funeral? [Understanding]

(a) To mourn his friend's death.
(b) To gain Brutus and Cassius's trust.
(c) To pitch his name as Caesar's successor.
(d) To unmask the conspirators.

(iii) 'Villians, you did not so, when your vile daggers
Hack'd one another in the sides of Caesar.'
Who is the speaker of these lines? [Recall]

(a) Cassius
(b) Brutus
(c) Octavius
(d) Antony

(iv) What dream did Cinna, the poet, have? [Recall]

(a) He was feasting with Caesar.
(b) He was killed by Caesar.
(c) He got an award for his poems.
(d) He was pelted by the crowd.

(v) 'His life was gentle, and the <u>elements</u>.'
Which of the following best describes the underlined word from *Julius Caesar*, Act V Scene 5? [Understanding]

(a) Privileged
(b) Advantages
(c) Comedy
(d) Memories

(vi) Antony wants to .... Caesar's will. [Understanding]

(a) Destroy
(b) Carry out
(c) Alter
(d) None of these

(vii) What two worlds are connected by the 'bridge of light' according to the poem 'Haunted Houses'? [Recall]

(a) Past and Future
(b) Heaven and Hell
(c) Earth and Jupiter
(d) Spirits and Humans

(viii) 'Cower down in desperation to accept
Whatever I accorded it to fate'
Which word from the above lines from the poem 'A Considerable Speck' means 'crouches'? [Understanding]

(a) Accept
(b) Desperation
(c) Accorded
(d) Cower

(ix) In the poem 'The Glove and the Lions' Count de Lorge bowed .... before the lady before leaping into the pit. [Understanding]

(a) Hesitantly
(b) Angrily
(c) Gracefully
(d) Quickly

(x) Choose the option that lists the sequence of events from Sukumar Ray's poem 'The Power of Music' in the correct order. [Recall]

I. People request Bhisma Lochan Sharma to stop his singing as the people thought they might depart this life.
II. The summer arrives.
III. Trees and buildings in the village start to fall and collapse.
IV. Bhisma's loud and powerful singing can be heard unwaveringly from Delhi to Burma.

(a) III, II, I and IV
(b) II, III, I and IV
(c) I, IV, II and III
(d) II, IV, III and I

(xi) 'Our eyes, briefly,
see with
a hurtful clarity'
What is the meaning of hurtful clarity in the above lines taken from Maya Angelou's poem 'When Great Trees fall'? [Understanding]

(a) Horrifying diseases
(b) Occasional loss
(c) Painful memories
(d) Getting a reality check

(xii) How does Martin describe the creepy lady's cheeks in the short story 'The Elevator'? [Recall]

(a) Fleshy (b) Chubby (c) Rosy (d) Prickly

(xiii) Who is the author of the story 'With the Photographer'? [Recall]

(a) Robert Frost
(b) Stephen Leacock
(c) Stephen Sleator
(d) Vikram Seth

(xiv) What award did Adjoa win in the short story 'The Girl Who Can'? **[Recall]**

(a) Best all-round junior athlete.
(b) Best junior girl athlete.
(c) Best all-round senior athlete.
(d) She didn't win anything.

(xv) Select the option that shows the correct relationship between Statements (I) and (II) from Alphonse Daudet's short story 'The Last Lesson'. **[Analysis]**

Statement I Franz after seeing the plight of his teacher, M. Hamel suddenly developed love and respect for him and his unwavering service to the school.

Statement II After hearing his teacher's new announcement, Franz realised that M. Hamel will not teach him French anymore.

(a) I and II are dependent on each other.
(b) I is the cause for II.
(c) II is the cause for I.
(d) I and II are independent of each other.

(xvi) What does Mr. Mead say about his family life in Ray Bradbury's short story 'The Pedestrian'? **[Understanding]**

(a) He says he is a widower.
(b) He says he is single.
(c) He says he is seeing someone special.
(d) He says he lives with his mother.

Section B (Answer one or more questions from the Section)

DRAMA

Julius Caesar

By William Shakespeare

Question 2.

Read the extract given below and answer the questions that follow.

Cassius : Messala, This is my birthday; as this very day
Was Cassius born. Give me thy hand, Messala:
Be thou my witness that against my will,
As Pompey was, am I compell'd to set
Upon one battle all our liberties.
You know that I held Epicurus strong
And his opinion: now I change my mind,
And partly credit things that do presage.
Coming from Sardis, on our former ensign
Two mighty eagles fell, and there they perch'd,
Gorging and feeding from our soldiers' hands;
Who to Philippi here consorted us:
This morning are they fled away and gone
And in their steads do ravens, crows, and kites,
Fly o'er our heads and downward look on us,
As we were sickly prey: their shadows seem
A canopy most fatal, under which
Our army lies, ready to give up the ghost.

(i) What occasion are they celebrating in the above lines?

Who does Cassius share this occasion with?

What compromise does he have to make? [Recall and Understanding] (3)

(ii) What event does Cassius share his sentiments about?

Explain his feelings. [Recall and Understanding] (3)

(iii) What were Cassius initial beliefs?

Why has his perspective changed now? [Recall and Understanding] (3)

(iv) What omen does Cassius see?

What do the 'ravens' represent? [Recall] (3)

(v) Does Cassius believe the signs are a bad omen?

Do you agree? [Analysis] (4)

Question 3.

Read the extract given below and answer the questions that follow.

Titinius : No, this was he Messala,
But Cassius is no more. O setting sun,
As in thy red rays thou dost sink to-night,
So in his red blood Cassius' day is set;
The sun of Rome is set! Our day is gone;
Clouds, dews, and dangers come; our deeds are done!
Mistrust of my success hath done this deed.

Messala : Mistrust of good success hath done this deed.
O hateful error, melancholy's child,
Why dost thou show to the apt thoughts of men
The things that are not? O error, soon conceived,
Thou never comest unto a happy birth,
But kill'st the mother that engender'd thee!

(i) What major event precedes this conversation?

Why did Pindarus run away? [Recall and Understanding] (3)

(ii) 'Clouds, dews, and dangers come; our deeds are done!'

What do 'deeds' refer to?

Was Cassius death related to the said 'deed'? [Recall] (3)

(iii) According to Messala, what are the dangers of mistrust?

How does it affect one's judgment? [Recall and Understanding] (3)

(iv) Who are Messala and Titinius looking for? Why?

Are they able to find him/her? [Recall] (3)

(v) How does Titinius describe Cassius death?

What does he do in his grief? [Recall and Understanding] (4)

Section C (Answer one or more questions from this Section)

PROSE-SHORT STORIES

(Treasure Chest - A Collection of ICSE Short Stories and Poems)

Question 4.

Read the following extract from Ama Ata Aidoo's short story 'The Girl Who Can' and answer the questions that follow.

But then Nana herself looked so pleased, out of surprise my mother shut her mouth up. In any case, since the first time they heard the news, I have often caught Nana staring at my legs with a strange look on her face, but still pretending like she was not looking. All this week, she has been washing my school uniform herself. That is a big surprise. And she didn't stop at that, she even went to Mr Mensah's house and borrowed his charcoal pressing iron each time, came back home with it, and ironed and ironed the uniform, until, if I had been the uniform, I would have said aloud that I had had enough.

(i) Who is Kaya?

What news do Kaya and Nana hear?

What is the news about? **[Recall] (3)**

(ii) What was the importance of legs according to Nana initially?

Why was she staring strangely at Adjoa's legs? **[Recall and Understanding] (3)**

(iii) Why was Nana pleased with the news she learned? **[Understanding] (3)**

(iv) What did Nana do after hearing the news?

How did Adjoa feel about her actions? **[Recall and Understanding] (3)**

(v) What does this incident tell us about Nana? **[Analysis] (4)**

Question 5.

Read the following extract from Alphonse Daudet's short story 'The Last Lesson' and answer the questions that follow.

But nothing happened, M. Hamel saw me and said very kindly, "Go to your place quickly, little Franz. We were beginning without you." I jumped over the bench and sat down at my desk. Not till then, when I had got a little over my fright, did I see that our teacher had on his beautiful green coat, his frilled shirt, and the little black silk cap, all embroidered, that he never wore except on inspection and prize days. Besides, the whole school seemed so strange and solemn.

SP-04

(i) Why was Franz late to school?

What did he expect M. Hamel to do when he arrived?

Was he correct? **[Recall and Understanding] (3)**

(ii) What was M. Hamel wearing that day?

Why was it unusual? **[Recall and Understanding] (3)**

(iii) 'Besides, the whole school seemed so strange and solemn.' Why? **[Understanding] (3)**

(iv) Who all were sitting in the class that day?

Why were they sitting in the class? **[Recall and Understanding] (3)**

(v) How was M. Hamel's temperament that day?

Was it different from his usual behaviour?

Why? **[Understanding and Analysis] (4)**

Section D (Answer one or more questions from this Section)

POETRY

(Treasure Chest - A Collection of ICSE SHort Stories and Poems)

Question 6.

Read the following extract from Robert Frost's poem 'A Considerable Speck' and answer the questions that follow.

This was no dust speck by my breathing blown,
But unmistakably a living mite
With inclinations it could call its own.
It paused as with suspicion of my pen,
And then came racing wildly on again
To where my manuscript was not yet dry;
Then paused again and drank or smelt-
With loathing, for again it turned to fly.

(i) What did the poet wrongly observe about the speck? [Recall] (3)

(ii) Why did the mite fly away again? [Understanding] (3)

(iii) 'It paused as with suspicion of my pen'

Why did the speck pause? [Understanding] (3)

(iv) What did the mite do around the ink? [Recall] (3)

(v) What does the word 'inclinations' mean in the context of the poem? [Analysis] (4)

Question 7.

Read the following extract from Sukuma Ray's poem 'The Power of Music' and answer the questions that follow.

The wretched brutes resent the blare the hour
they heard it sounded,
They whine and stare with feet in air or wonder
quite confounded.
The fishes dived below the lake in frantic search
for silence,
The very trees collapse and shake - you hear the
crash a mile hence -

(i) Who are 'the wretched brutes'? [Recall] (3)

(ii) What actions did the animals take in the above lines to escape the sound? [Recall] (3)

(iii) Why do the fish dive to the bottom of the lake? [Understanding] (3)

(iv) Explain the meaning of the following phrases: [Understanding] (3)

(a) Resent the blare

(b) Confounded

(c) Frantic Search

(v) What is the cause of animals' distress? How does it affect humans and trees? [Recall and Understanding] (4)

Answers in Topper's Style

1. (i) (c) For not defending Pella.
   (ii) (d) To unmask the conspirators.
   (iii) (d) Antony
   (iv) (a) He was feasting with Caesar.
   (v) (c) Comedy
   (vi) (c) Alter
   (vii) (d) Spirits and Humans
   (viii) (d) Cower
   (ix) (c) Gracefully
   (x) (d) II, IV, III and I
   (xi) (b) Occasional loss
   (xii) (a) Fleshy
   (xiii) (b) Stephen Leacock
   (xiv) (a) Best all-round junior athlete.
   (xv) (c) II is the cause for I.
   (xvi) (b) He says he is single.

2. (i) They are celebrating Cassius birthday in the given lines.

   Cassius is sharing this event with Messala.

   He admits to adhere to Epicurus' philosophy and didn't generally believe in omens. But the recent sighting of ravens over his army has given space to doubts in his head. He expresses his confusion between his beliefs and instincts of impending doom.

   (ii) Cassius is worried about the outcome of the upcoming battle.

   He is unwilling to stake everything on its outcome. He compares himself to Pompey, someone who had to risk everything during a civil war against Caesar.

   (iii) Cassius was initially an admirer of Epicurus and his philosophies. Epicurus didn't believe in the impact of the supernatural on a human life. He expressed strong disbelief in signs and omens.

   Cassius changed his perspective as he was unhappy with the consequence of his choices. His actions had led him into a massive civil war that he didn't want to participate in anymore.

   (iv) Cassius witnesses two eagles land on their flag when he and Brutus were enroute to Philippi. The eagles were friendly with the soldiers and ate from their hands. But, after arriving at Philippi, the eagles were nowhere to be seen. Instead, Cassius saw birds of prey like ravens and crows replace the eagles. They would hover over their army base. The birds' shadow would look like dark clouds hovering over the army, as if it was waiting for them to die.

   The 'ravens' represent a bird of prey. Their presence represents a warning of the impending danger to Cassius army.

   (v) Cassius generally doesn't trust omens or signs. But he is struggling to deny the recent signs he witnessed as predictions of disaster. The replacement of eagles with ravens had made Cassius question his own beliefs.

   I believe that the signs in this scene were a bad omen. It foreshadows the results of the battle at Philippi. Brutus and Cassius army loses and Cassius eventually commits suicide.

3. (i) Cassius suicide precedes this conversation.

   Pindarus, Cassius servant, had killed his master on the latter's instruction. This act grants him his freedom but also the guilt of murdering his master overwhelms him. He finds this burden heavier than servitude. He is afraid of judgment and the consequence of his actions that will land him in trouble. So, he flees before he is judged.

   (ii) The 'deeds' refer to Titinius' mission. He was tasked with a responsibility to learn whether the tents were set up by their friends or foes.

   Yes, Cassius's death was related to the said 'deeds'. The uncertainty of the mission's outcome led Cassius to feel sad and anxious. This drove him to commit suicide later.

   (iii) Messala interprets mistrust can give rise to incorrect thoughts and ideas. It could cloud a person's instinct and decisions immensely. It had the capacity to ruin a person.

   One's judgment can be hindered when engulfed in paranoia and can lead them to make rash decisions.

(iv) Messala and Titinius are looking for Pindarus. He was the last individual to see Cassius alive. They want to understand the sequential order of events that resulted in Cassius's death.

They are unable to find him as he decided to run far away so that no Roman could ever find him.

(v) Titinius compares Cassius body to the sunset. He draws the similarity in hues of red that paint the sky during sunset to pools of blood that are scattered around Cassius corpse. Just like the red in the sky denotes the end of the day, Cassius's blood around him also signifies the termination of his life.

Titinius, overwhelmed by the grief of losing his dear friend, commits suicide.

4. (i) Kaya is Adjoa's mother or Maami.

The news they hear is about Adjoa.

Kaya and Nana learn about Adjoa's selection as an athlete in the junior level of the district games.

(ii) Initially, Nana believed that legs are crucial for supporting a woman for child bearing. She postulates that women with strong legs are the only ones capable of bearing healthy children. As Adjoa had thin legs, Nana complains that they will be too weak for any use.

After hearing about Adjoa's selection in the district games, Nana stares strangely at Adjoa's legs as she is puzzled by Adjoa's selection. She is astonished at the possibility that Adjoa's 'weak' and 'thin' legs could be useful.

(iii) Regardless of her earlier reservations, Nana is pleased with Adjoa's selection as an athlete. She is proud of Adjoa for proving her wrong and enlightening her to the many other uses and importance of legs.

(iv) Nana washes and irons Adjoa's uniform everyday herself for the entire week of Adjoa's games. She even borrows the charcoal iron for Mr. Mensah to ensure Adjoa looks her best while participating in the games.

Adjoa is surprised by her actions as, before her selection, Nana had been the biggest opposer of Adjoa's education.

(v) The incident depicts Nana's love for her granddaughter. It displayed her capacity to show care and acknowledgement of Adjoa's achievements. She is proud of her granddaughter's accomplishment and shows it in her own subtle ways. She washes and irons her uniform to ensure Adjoa feels her best while performing. Even though she displayed her skepticism towards Adjoa's education and appearance in the past, she is capable of leaving her old ideas behind and supporting Adjoa in her endeavors.

5. (i) Franz was late to school as he dreaded facing M. Hamel that morning. He had forgotten to practice his participles and feared receiving punishment for his carelessness.

He expected M. Hamel to reprimand him for being late.

No, he was incorrect. M. Hamel surprised him by acting gentle towards him.

(ii) M. Hamel was wearing a beautiful green coat, a shirt with frills and a black silk cap.

This was unusual to Franz as it was Hamel's fanciest attire, which he only wore on special occasions. Franz failed to understand why M. Hamel was wearing his fancy attire on a regular day.

(iii) The whole school looked sad as a new order had come from Berlin to discontinue teaching French in the schools of Alsace from the next day. M. Hamel, being a French language teacher, would no longer be allowed to teach his subject. Thus, he was leaving the next day, making it his last day at school. After forty years of service, everyone was devastated to see him leave so suddenly.

(iv) All the villagers including old Hauser, the former mayor and postmaster of the village were sitting at the back benches of the class that day.

They came to show appreciation for M. Hamel's dedication to the school. They were remorseful for not comprehending his importance before. They wanted to attend his lesson one last time and show their respect for him and love for their language.

(v) M. Hamel's demeanor was calm and gentle that day.

This was different from his usual temperament. He would often quickly express anger and lose patience with his students. However, today, he was quiet and patient. He taught the students and villagers with utmost compassion and dedication.

He was upset about losing his job of forty years. The annexation of Alsace by Germany led to a new law of replacing French with German language. This forced him to leave the life and place he knew behind into the unknown future.

6. (i) The poet mistook the mite as a speck of dust.
   (ii) After realising that the ink drops are harmful, the mite is sickened by it and decides to flee and save himself by flying away.
   (iii) The speck was attempting to find a way to safety. It pauses to inspect the pen that may be an obstacle for it on the paper before walking near it.
   (iv) The mite is trying to save its life. It stops to inspect the drops of ink as it is both curious and suspicious of its nature. So, it smelt and tasted the ink before deciding its poisonous effect.
   (v) 'Inclination' means the natural tendency to feel or act a certain way. In the poem, the word is used to denote the mite's natural tendency to use his brain and form an idea or opinion of its own regardless of the size of its existence.

7. (i) The beasts or animals are referred to as 'brutes'. They are 'wretched' as they are in agony from bearing Bhisma's singing.
   (ii) The animals are upset with Bhisma's loud and continuous singing. They show their annoyance by screaming loudly. Some animals cry loudly and sit with their legs in the air to express their annoyance. Fishes dive deep into the lake to escape his singing.
   (iii) The fish try to distance themselves from the surface of the lake to escape Bhisma's forceful singing. They go to the lake's bottom to search for a silent corner to enjoy.
   (iv) (a) Dislike for loud noises
   (b) Confused
   (c) Agitated lookout
   (v) Animals are distressed by Bhisma's continuous singing. They are agitated by the volume and power of his voice leading them to act abnormally. Bhisma's stubbornness for singing without any regard for the well-being of his neighbours and surrounding, has drained animals and humans alike.

   People have requested Bhisma to cease his singing. They believe they might die if they had to endure his singing for another minute. The trees far away shake and collapse by the raw strength of Bhisma's voice.

SQP Code : **PB-5/10**

Series ***i*-Succeed 5-25/10**

Roll No.

Sample Question Paper 05

Literature in English 10th (Code 01)

General Instructions

1. You will not be allowed to write during the first 15 minutes. This time is to be spent in reading the question paper.
2. The time given at the head of this paper is the time allowed for writing the answers.
3. The paper has four Sections.
4. Section A is compulsory - All questions in Section A must be answered.
5. You must attempt one question from each of the Sections B, C and D and one other question from any section of your choice.
6. The intended marks for questions or parts of questions are given in brackets [ ].

Time : 2 Hrs.

Max. Marks : 80

Section A (Attempt all questions from this Section)

Question 1.

Choose the correct answer to the questions from the given options. (16)

(i) What does Caesar's ghost tell Brutus? [Recall]

(a) Brutus will die a cruel death.
(b) He will see Brutus in Philippi.
(c) Brutus will be betrayed by Lucilius.
(d) He will see Brutus in hell.

(ii) .... accuses .... for taking bribes. [Recall]

(a) Brutus, Lucilius
(b) Lucilius, Cassius
(c) Cassius, Lucilius
(d) Brutus, Cassius

(iii) Which of the following does Brutus think Cassius has done? [Recall]

(a) Take bribes from corrupt men
(b) Betrayed Rome
(c) Has become slightly cold towards Brutus and Lucilius
(d) All of the above

(iv) What quality did Caesar have from the following options? [Understanding]

(a) Leadership
(b) Cowardice
(c) Humour
(d) Naivety

(v) 'Then, if we lose this battle,

You are contented to be led in triumph
Thorough the streets of Rome' ?
Who is 'You'? [Recall]

(a) Cassius (b) Antony
(c) Brutus (d) Lucilius

(vi) Why did Brutus join the conspiracy? [Understanding]

(a) He was scared of being killed by other conspirators.
(b) He wanted to become the new leader of Rome.
(c) He thought it was an honourable thing to do.
(d) None of the above

(vii) Choose the option that lists the sequence of events from Robert Frost's poem 'A Considerable Speck' in the correct order. [Recall]

I. The mite runs to the middle of the white paper.
II. The poet waits for the mite to fall asleep.
III. The mite halts and smells the ink.
IV. The poet wants to erase the mite using the ink.

(a) IV, III, I and II (b) I, IV, III and II
(c) I, IV, II and III (d) I, III, IV and II

(viii) Select the word that best describes the King from the poem 'The Glove and the Lions'. [Understanding]

I. Lively II. Daring III. Energetic IV. Lazy

(a) I and III (b) I and IV (c) II and III (d) II and IV

(ix) How did Bhisma sing in Sukumar Ray's poem 'The Power of Music'? [Understanding]

(a) Loud and Beautiful (b) Soft and Beautiful
(c) Loud and Powerful (d) Soft and Powerful

(x) How can we honour the great souls after they leave us according to the poem 'When Great Trees fall'? [Understanding]

(a) Celebrating their birthday (b) Forgetting their existence
(c) Talking bad about them (d) Trying to be better people

SP-05

(xi) 'Wander our thoughts above the dark abyss'

What does the word 'abyss' mean in the above line from the poem 'Haunted Houses'? [Recall]

(a) Uncharted territory (b) Bottomless pit
(c) Forest field (d) Night sky

(xii) What best describes Ray Bradbury's short story 'The Pedestrian'? [Understanding]

(a) Fairy Tale (b) Dream
(c) Sci-fi story (d) Dystopian Tale

(xiii) The short story 'The Last Lesson' symbolises [Understanding]

(a) importance of the French language. (b) importance of schools.
(c) importance of education and language. (d) importance of goodbyes.

(xiv) How old is Martin in William Sleator's short story 'The Elevator'? [Recall]

(a) 10 (b) 12 (c) 15 (d) 7

(xv) In the short story 'With the Photographer', what did the author compare the photographer's dim eye with? [Recall]

(a) Natural Scientist
(b) Abstract Artist
(c) Beautiful Dancer
(d) Dingy Chandelier

(xvi) Select the option that shows the correct relationship between Statements (I) and (II) from Ama Ata Aidoo's short story 'The Girl Who Can'. [Analysis]

Statement I Nana criticised Adjoa's legs for being thin and not strong enough to run long distances.

Statement II Nana criticised Adjoa's legs for being thin and not strong enough for child bearing.

(a) I is true and II is false .
(b) II is true and I is false.
(c) I is the cause for II.
(d) I and II are independent of each other.

Section B (Answer one or more questions from this Section)

DRAMA

Julius Caesar

By William Shakespeare

Question 2.

Read the extract given below and answer the questions that follow.

Antony	:	Octavius, lead your battle softly on,
	:	Upon the left hand of the even field.
Octavius	:	Upon the right hand I; keep thou the left.
Antony	:	Why do you cross me in this exigent?
Octavius	:	I do not cross you; but i will do so. March.
Brutus	:	They stand, and would have parley.
Cassius	:	Stand fast, Titinius: we must out and talk.
Octavius	:	Mark Antony, shall we give sign of battle?
Antony	:	No, Caesar, we will answer on their charge.
		Make forth; the generals would have some words.

(i) Where does the above scene take place?
Briefly describe the setting of the above scene. [Understanding] (3)

(ii) What strategy does Antony suggest for the battle?
Does Octavius agree with his approach? [Recall] (3)

(iii) Who is Octavius?
Why does he want to establish by agreeing/disagreeing with Antony? [Recall and Understanding] (3)

(iv) What do Brutus and Cassius see in the above scene?
What conclusion do they arrive at? [Recall and Understanding] (3)

(v) What decision was made on both sides in this scene?
Was it able to resolve the problems between them? [Recall and Understanding] (4)

Question 3.

Read the extract given below and answer the questions that follow.

Fourth Citizen : It is no matter, his name's Cinna; pluck but his name out of his heart, and turn him going.

Third Citizen : Tear him, tear him! Come, brands ho! firebrands: to Brutus' to Cassius'; burn all: some to Decius' house, and some to Casca's; some to Ligarius': away, go!

(i) Which scene from *Julius Caesar* are these lines from?
Briefly explain what happened before this scene. [Recall and Understanding] (3)

(ii) Why does the fourth citizen get angry when he hears the man they have is named Cinna?
What do they decide to do with him? [Analysis and Understanding] (3)

(iii) Is Cinna the same as the one the crowd was looking for?
If not, does the crowd spare him? [Recall] (3)

(iv) What do the citizens use to wreak havoc in the city?
Whose houses do they plan to destroy using it? [Recall] (3)

(v) Why was the crowd so aggravated?
What does the incident with Cinna say about the plight of Rome? [Recall and Understanding] (4)

Section C (Answer one or more questions from this Section)

PROSE-SHORT STORIES

(Treasure Chest - A Collection of ICSE Short Stories and Poems)

Question 4.

SP-05

Read the following extract from Ray Bradbury's short story 'The Pedestrian' and answer the questions that follow.

He walked like a man suddenly drunk. As he passed the front window of the car he looked in. As he had expected, there was no one in the front seat, no one in the car at all. "Get in." He put his hand to the door and peered into the back seat, which was a little cell, a little black jail with bars. It smelled of riveted steel. It smelled of harsh antiseptic; it smelled too clean and hard and metallic. There was nothing soft there.

"Now if you had a wife to give you an alibi," said the iron voice. "But -"

"Where are you taking me?" The car hesitated, or rather gave a faint whirring click, as if information, somewhere, was dropping card by punch-slotted card under electric eyes. "To the Psychiatric Center for Research on Regressive Tendencies."

He got in. The door shut with a soft thud.

The police car rolled through the night avenues, flashing its dim lights ahead.

They passed one house on one street a moment later, one house in an entire city of houses that were dark, but this one particular house had all of its electric lights brightly lit, every window a loud yellow illumination, square and warm in the cool darkness.

(i) What car did Mr. Mead gets inside?
Was there anyone inside the car?
What does he see when he sits inside it? [Recall and Understanding] (3)

(ii) Why was Mr. Mead arrested?
What could have saved him according to the police? [Recall and Understanding] (3)

(iii) Where was Mr. Mead being taken to? Why? [Recall and Understanding] (3)

(iv) What did Mr. Mead see on the way to his destination?
Does the car acknowledge it too? [Recall] (3)

(v) Use one word to describe the type of world the above story is based on.
What issues does the author plan to highlight in this story? [Analysis and Understanding] (4)

Question 5.

Read the following extract from Alphonse Daudet's short story 'The Last Lesson' and answer the questions that follow.

Oh, how sorry I was for not learning my lessons, for seeking bird's eggs or going sliding on the Saar! My books, that had seemed such a nuisance a while ago, so heavy to carry, my grammar, and my history of the saints, were old friends now that I couldn't give up. And M. Hamel, too; the idea that he was going away, that I should never see him again, made me forget all about his ruler and how cranky he was. Poor man! It was an honour of this last lesson that he had put on his fine Sunday-clothes, and now I understood why the old men of the village were sitting there in the back of the room.

(i) What did M. Hamel announce to the class?
Why did he make this decision?
How did he feel about his decision? [Recall and Understanding] (3)

(ii) How did little Franz feel after hearing M. Hamel's news?
What did he regret? [Recall and Understanding] (3)

(iii) How did M. Hamel behave with Franz before that day? [Understanding] (3)

(iv) Why were the old men of the village sitting at the back of the room?
Was that a usual occurrence? [Analysis and Understanding] (3)

(v) What was M. Hamel wearing for that day?
Why is it unusual?
If not, why did he decide to wear them today? [Recall and Evaluative] (4)

SP-05

Section D (Answer one or more questions from this Section)

POETRY

(Treasure Chest - A Collection of ICSE Short Stories and Poems)

Question 6.

Read the following extract from Sukumar Ray's poem 'The Power of Music' and answer the questions that follow.

When summer comes, we hear the hums
Bhisma Lochan Kumar

You catch his strain on hill and plain from Delhi
down to Burma
He sings as though he's staked his life, he sings
as though he's hell-bent;
The people, dazed, retire amazed although they
know it's well-meant.

(i) Who is the protagonist of the poem? [Recall] (3)

(ii) What qualities of the protagonist the people despise? [Recall] (3)

(iii) The protagonist is 'hell-bent' on showcasing his talent. Why? [Understanding] (3)

(iv) The protagonist showcases his talent boldly. How famous is he for it?
How do people respond when he showcases his talent? [Understanding] (3)

(v) What personality traits of the protagonist are highlighted in the above lines? [Understanding] (4)

Question 7.

Read the following extract from Leigh Hunt's poem 'The Glove and the Lions' and answer the questions that follow.

King Francis was a heart king, and loved a royal sport,
And one day as his lions fought, sat looking on the court;
The nobles filled the benches, and the ladies in their pride,
And 'mongst them sat the Count de Lorge, with one for whom he sighed:
And truly 'twas a gallant thing to see that crowning show,
Valour and love, and a king above, and the royal beasts below.

(i) What adjective does the poet use to describe the following? [Recall] (3)

(a) The event

(b) The participants of the event

(ii) Who did the king sigh for and what quality of ladies has the poet highlighted in the poem? [Recall] (3)

SP-05

(iii) Later, what does Count's Lover do to lose the King's favour? [Recall] (3)

(iv) Where is the above incident taking place?
Who all are present?
What type of king was King Francis? [Recall and Understanding] (3)

(v) What type of poetic device is used on 'Lions fought'? Elaborate on its use. [Understanding and Analysis] (4)

Answers in Topper's Style

1. (i) (b) He will see Brutus in Philippi.
   (ii) (d) Brutus, Cassius
   (iii) (d) All of the above
   (iv) (a) Leadership
   (v) (c) Brutus
   (vi) (c) He thought it was an honourable thing to do.
   (vii) (a) IV, III, I and II
   (viii) (a) I and III
   (ix) (c) Loud and Powerful
   (x) (d) Trying to be better people
   (xi) (a) Uncharted territory
   (xii) (d) Dystopian Tale
   (xiii) (c) importance of education and language.
   (xiv) (b) 12
   (xv) (a) Natural Scientist
   (xvi) (b) II is true and I is false.

2. (i) The above scene takes place in Philippi.

   In the scene, Brutus and Cassius' army is marching towards Antony and Octavius' army in Philippi. On receiving a message confirming Brutus and Cassius' advances, Antony and Octavius are arguing about their strategy.

   (ii) Antony tells Octavius to softly lead his army on the left side of the field while he would take his army to the right side.

   Octavius disagrees with him and declares his intentions to approach from the right side of the field and asks Antony to take the left side.

   (iii) Octavius Caesar is Caesar's nephew. He is the heir to Caesar's empire and the next rightful general of Rome based on hierarchy.

   Octavius disagrees with Antony's strategies as he wants to assert his authority over Antony. He defies his command to establish his leadership and independence. He doesn't want to follow Antony's directive to strengthen his claim to power after Caesar.

   (iv) When Brutus and Cassius army reach the field, they observe that their opponents were waiting and not advancing towards them for battle.

   From this, they deduced that Antony and Octavius wanted a word with them prior to the battle.

   (v) The generals from both the sides decided to converse in private, prior to the war. They instructed their respective soldiers to not attack unless they signal. Then, they proceed to meet in the middle of the field to talk.

   No, they are unable to resolve the problems between them. Instead, they end up insulting each other and go forward with their plans to battle.

3. (i) These lines are from Act III, Scene 3 of *Julius Caesar*.

   Before this scene, Antony addressed the crowds at Caesar's Funeral. He unmasks the conspirators behind Caesar's assassination. The crowd realises the injustice Caesar faced and mourn the loss of their great Roman leader. It also enrages the plebeians and they charge off to wreak havoc around the city to seek revenge from the conspirators.

   (ii) Cinna was the name of one of the conspirators behind Caesar's assassination. This enrages the fourth citizen as he is one of the plebeians seeking justice for his beloved leader.

   Initially, they decide to let him go. But, later their anger escalates and they decide to tear him apart instead.

   (iii) No, the Cinna they caught was Cinna, the poet and not Cinna, the conspirator.

   No, the crowd didn't spare him. Even though they realised he was innocent, the mob's anger superseded their logical thinking and they ended up beating him to death.

   (iv) The citizens plan to use firebrands to wreak havoc in the city.

   They target houses of conspirators like Brutus, Cassius, Decius, Casca and Ligarius. They plan to burn and destroy their houses using the firebrands.

   (v) The crowd was displeased about Caesar's assassination. After Antony's speech, they realised that Caesar was a great leader who was betrayed by his own men. They were aggravated after losing their general and were thirsty for revenge.

   Cinna's pointless murder indicates the start of rebellion and civil war in Rome. With the demise of Caesar, the city is filled with fear, speculation and disorder. The plebeians have become vulnerable after the loss of their protector and are easy to manipulate to commit acts of retribution.

Lawlessness has plagued the streets of Rome which indicates more commotion that is yet to come.

4. (i) Mr. Mead gets inside a police car.

No one was inside the car when Mr. Mead got in. He sees that car was working on its own and observed that the backseat of the car was like a little black jail with bars. It smelled like riveting steel and antiseptic. It smelled too clean, hard and metallic. Nothing felt soft inside.

(ii) Mr. Mead was arrested for walking alone in the evening on an isolated street. In the year 2053, the society had become technology driven. People spend their evenings at home watching television. It was unusual to see anyone on the street at that time of the day.

According to the police car, Mr. Mead could have been saved if he had a wife to give an alibi in his favour.

(iii) Mr. Mead was being taken to the Psychiatric Center for Research on Regressive Tendencies. In the year 2053, the world is technologically dependent. People are addicted to television and spend most of the time with their eyes glued to the screen. Mr. Mead's unconventional practice of walking on the streets at night was different from the norm. His preference for natural human experiences over the technologically stimulated ones were concluded to be regressive and potentially dangerous by the police car. Hence, he was taken to such a facility.

(iv) Mr. Mead saw his house on their way to the psychiatric center. Mr. Mead's house was the only one that had electric lights and was lit up.

When he pointed at his house, the car paid no heed to his comment and kept driving.

(v) The best word to describe the world Ray Bradbury creates in his story is 'Dystopian'.

The story sheds a light on the dangers of overdependence on technology in today's world. With new advancements, most manual jobs have been replaced by machines. Technology has made work simpler, faster and more efficient. However, it also led to people becoming lazy and addicted. In the world that Bradbury describes, the society is technologically-ruled, dehumanising some part of their existence. People are addicted to television and human interactions have become minimal. Mr. Mead, the protagonist, is the symbol of soul and humanity by not conforming to this new norm. Through his story, Bradbury tries to display an admonishing tale, which warns the world of the disadvantages of becoming technologically driven. He predicts that such a society would mean a loss of individuality, creativity and autonomy.

5. (i) M. Hamel announced that he would be teaching his last French lesson in Alsace that day.

He was forced to make this decision. French cities, Alsace and Lorraine, were recently occupied by Germany. They had issued the directive to teach only German in their schools. This had made M. Hamel's job as a French teacher futile and, so, he had to leave.

He was devastated and emotional about his decision. He served as a French teacher for the last forty years. He loved his occupation and was a patriot at heart. So the idea of leaving his country had greatly upset him.

(ii) M. Hamel's news felt like a thunderclap to Franz. He was shocked by the abrupt revelation. He was also saddened to see his teacher go.

He regretted not paying attention to his lessons. He wished he had learned his lessons instead of going egg hunting or sliding at Saar. He realised the importance of his language and how he had taken it for granted.

(iii) M. Hamel was a strict teacher. Before that day, he used to behave crankily with Franz.

Franz also implies that Hamel often used to punish mischievous students by hitting them with his ruler.

(iv) The old men of the village were sitting at the back of the room as a sign of respect towards M. Hamel's service to the school. They were remorseful to see him go and for taking his lessons for granted over the years. They wanted to honour his dedication by attending his last lesson.

Hence, no, the old men attending the lesson was not a usual occurrence at the school.

(v) M. Hamel was wearing his fine Sunday clothes. It consisted of his beautiful green coat, frilled shirt with a black silk embroidered cap.

It was unusual for him to dress fancy on a normal school day. He was known to only wear them on special occasions.

He decided to wear the clothes as this was his last lesson at the school. He was devastated knowing he was leaving soon. So, he wore his best dress to mark this momentous but sad occasion.

6. (i) Bhisma Lochan Kumar is a singer and the protagonist of the poem.

(ii) The people despise Bhisma's loud and continuous singing. They also hate his ignorance of their plight. Even after requesting him to stop his singing to gain some peace, Bhisma refuses to acknowledge their request and keeps singing.

(iii) Bhisma is 'hell-bent' on showcasing his talent as he refuses to halt his singing for anyone. Instead, he sings as powerfully as he can as if his life depends on it.

(iv) Bhisma is very famous for his singing. The poet highlights that whenever summer arrives, Bhisma starts to sing. His voice is so potent and voluminous that it can be heard from Delhi to Burma.

Although the people recognise his talent, the force of his singing is so massive that they have grown tired of it. They are amazed by his talent and know he means well. However, they request him to stop his performance to gather some peace but to no avail.

(v) Bhisma is relentless and irritating at the same time. He is proud about his talent and has confidence to showcase it. However, he is also disrespectful and dismissive of everyone around him. His determination to display his talent is commendable. But his stubbornness to not stop even after several requests from his peers is irritating and unacceptable. His disregard for the well-being of others makes his singing and character unattractive.

7. (i) (a) Royal sport, crowning show

(b) Gallant thing, royal beasts

(ii) The King sighed after looking at the Count's lady love who is an attractive young woman.

The poem highlights the prideful nature that is displayed by the women present in the court. The poem later on also highlights the vanity and hollowness of their nature by using Count's Lady Love's actions as an example.

(iii) Count's Lady Love filled with the delusions of glory decides to test the Count's love for her. She throws her glove in the lion's pit and expectantly looks at the Count to retrieve it for her. She doesn't recognise the risk she is putting the Count in, only to fulfill her selfish need to establish her superiority. Her superficial and hollow act makes her lose the King's favour.

(iv) The lion's fight is taking place in the royal court of King Francis.

Many nobles and their ladies are present to witness the occasion.

King Francis is described as a jovial and light-hearted king.

(v) The poetic device in the above phrase is a metaphor. In the poem, the lions are pitted against each other to fight and kill each other for the entertainment of the King and his court. The 'lions' or 'beasts' also refer to the noblemen who are the subjects of the King. Like the lions, they are pitted against each other to win the King's praise and favour.

SQP Code : **PB-6/10**	Series ***i*-Succeed 6-25/10**	Roll No.							

Sample Question Paper 06

Literature in English 10th (Code 01)

General Instructions

1. You will not be allowed to write during the first 15 minutes. This time is to be spent in reading the question paper.
2. The time given at the head of this paper is the time allowed for writing the answers.
3. The paper has four Sections.
4. Section A is compulsory - All questions in Section A must be answered.
5. You must attempt one question from each of the Sections B, C and D and one other question from any section of your choice.
6. The intended marks for questions or parts of questions are given in brackets [ ].

Time : 2 Hrs.

Max. Marks : 80

Section A (Attempt all questions from this Section)

Question 1.

Choose the correct answer to the questions from the given options. **(16)**

(i) 'No Rome of safety for Octavius yet'. **[Understanding]**

What does the statement mean?

(a) Octavius was trying to protect Antony.

(b) Antony was hunting Octavius to kill him.

(c) Octavius was unsafe as he was the next heir to the throne.

(d) None of the above

(ii) What does Caesar's cloak on his dead body symbolise? **[Understanding]**

(a) Symbol of Caesar's demise
(b) Symbol of betrayal
(c) Symbol of triumph
(d) Symbol of Caesar's royalty

(iii) Antony thinks Lepidus is .... **[Understanding]**

(a) loyal
(b) naive
(c) brave
(d) insignificant

(iv) What ominous sign did Cassius see? **[Recall]**

(a) Two eagles circling around their heads
(b) Two eagles sitting on their flag
(c) Two eagles accepting food from the soldiers
(d) All of these

(v) Portia kills herself by .... [Recall]

(a) swallowing hot coal
(b) drinking poison
(c) jumping off a building
(d) asking her friend to stab her

(vi) Who does Brutus order to hand over the bills to the legions in Act IV Scene 2? [Recall]

(a) Cassius (b) Lepidus (c) Titinius (d) Messala

(vii) What does 'bridge of light' signify in the poem 'Haunted Houses'? [Understanding]

(a) A pathway of light
(b) A pathway between a soul and heaven
(c) A pathway to heaven
(d) A pathway between Earth and spirit world

(viii) Choose the option that lists the sequence of events from Leigh Hunt's poem 'The Glove and the Lions' in the correct order. [Recall]

I. The Count throws the glove at his lady's face, revealing his disdain.
II. King Francis commends the Count.
III. King Francis is watching a fight between ferocious lions.
IV. The Lady drops her glove in the lion pit.

(a) III, IV, I and II (b) III, IV, II and I (c) I, IV, II and III (d) I, III, IV and II

(ix) In the poem 'When Great Trees Fall', what does the poet regret after losing someone significant? [Recall]

(a) Unkept Promises
(b) Shared experiences
(c) Words unsaid
(d) Memories not made

(x) Robert Frost's poem 'A Considerable Speck' uses .... type of social commentary. [Understanding]

(a) metaphor (b) irony (c) satire (d) imagery

(xi) 'The fishes lived below the lake'

What does the above line from the poem 'The Power of Music' display? [Understanding]

(a) The fishes were searching for silence.
(b) The fishes were trying to escape Bhisma's singing.
(c) Both (a) and (b)
(d) None of the above

(xii) Select the option that shows the correct relationship between Statements (I) and (II) from Stephen Leacock's short story 'With the Photographer'. [Analysis]

Statement I The narrator did not agree with the photographer because he had accepted his outer appearance.

Statement II The narrator did not agree with the photographer because he knew he was embarrassed of his outer appearance.

(a) I is true and II is false.
(b) II is true and I is false.
(c) I is the cause for II.
(d) I and II are independent of each other.

(xiii) What was Martin's biggest fear in the short story 'The Elevator'? [Recall]

(a) Going down the stairs.
(b) Getting bullied at school.
(c) Getting scolded by his father.
(d) Getting stuck in an elevator.

(xiv) At the end of 'The Girl Who Can', Nana changed her opinion. What did she change her opinion about? [Recall]

(a) Women's education
(b) Kaya's partner choices
(c) Her granddaughter's legs
(d) Athletic Games

(xv) Why do 'Magazines and books don't sell anymore' in the year 2053 in the short story 'The Pedestrian'? [Analysis]

(a) Books were banned by the new government.
(b) Everything was available online now.
(c) Education was not considered important anymore.
(d) People prefer television shows to books now.

(xvi) What does writing 'Vive La France' on the blackboard signify? [Understanding]

(a) M. Hamel's patriotism
(b) The name of the new lesson
(c) Franz's love for the language
(d) None of these

Section B (Answer one or more questions from this Section)

DRAMA

Julius Caesar

By William Shakespeare

Question 2.

Read the extract given below and answer the questions that follow.

Brutus : How ill this taper burns! Ha! Who comes here?
I think it is the weakness of mine eyes
That shapes this monstrous apparition.
It comes upon me. Art thou any thing?
Art thou some god, some angel, or some devil,
That makes my blood cold and my hair to stare?
Speak to me thou art.

(i) Where is Brutus in the above scene?
Who does Brutus see? [Recall] (3)

(ii) How does Brutus feel after seeing the newcomer?
Select the line from the extract that explains his feelings. [Understanding] (3)

(iii) Was anyone else present in the above scene?
Did they interact with the newcomer? [Recall] (3)

(iv) What did the newcomer say to Brutus?
How did it make him feel? [Recall and Understanding] (3)

(v) Explain 'How ill this taper burns!'.
How does Brutus answer the question 'Art thou any thing'? [Evaluative and Analysis] (4)

Question 3.

Read the extract given below and answer the questions that follow.

Antony : He hath brought many captives home to Rome
Whose ransoms did the general coffers fill:
Did this in Caesar seem ambitious?
When that the poor have cried, Caesar hath wept;
Ambition should be made of sterner stuff:
Yet Brutus says he was ambitious;

SP-06

And Brutus is an honourable man.
You all did see that on the Lupercal
I thrice presented him a kingly crown,
Which he did thrice refuse. Was this ambition?

(i) 'He hath brought many captives home to Rome'
Who is 'He'?
Why is Antony talking about him? [Recall and Understanding] (3)

(ii) Who is Antony addressing his speech to?
What does he plan on accomplishing by doing so? [Recall and Understanding] (3)

(iii) When that the poor have cried, Caesar hath wept;
Ambition should be made of sterner stuff:
What do the above lines mean? Does this paint Caesar in a good light?
[Recall and Understanding] (3)

(iv) "I thrice presented him a kingly crown",
Which he did thrice refuse was this ambition?
Who presented the 'kingly crown' and to whom? [Recall] (3)

(v) How does Antony belittle Brutus? Why is he trying to do so? [Understanding and Analysis] (4)

Section C (Answer one or more questions from this Section)

PROSE-SHORT STORIES

(Treasure Chest - A Collection of ICSE Short Stories and Poems)

Question 4.

Read the following extract from Ray Bradbury's short story 'The Pedestrian' and answer the questions that follow.

Sometimes he would walk for hours and miles and return only at midnight to his house. And on his way he would see the cottages and homes with their dark windows, and it was not unequal to walking through a graveyard where only the faintest glimmers of firefly light appeared in flickers behind the windows. Sudden gray phantoms seemed to manifest upon inner room walls where a curtain was still undrawn against the night, or there were whisperings and murmurs where a window in a tomblike was still open.

Mr. Leonard Mead would pause, cock his head, listen, look and march on, his feet making no noise on the lumpy walk. For long ago, he had wisely changed to sneakers when strolling at night, because the dogs in the intermittent squad would parallel his journey with barkings if he wore hard heels.

(i) Who was the only being outside other than Mr. Mead?
How did he feel about them? Why? [Recall and Understanding] (3)

(ii) What does the author compare 'the cottages and homes' with? [Recall] (3)

(iii) What were Mr. Mead's thoughts as he walked past the houses? [Recall] (3)

(iv) Where was Mr. Mead headed that evening?
What did he see and feel? [Recall and Understanding] (3)

(v) What was Mr. Mead's unusual ritual?
How was he different from the rest of the city? [Recall and Understanding] (4)

Question 5.

Read the following extract from Alphonse Daudet's short story 'The Last Lesson' and answer the questions that follow.

While I was thinking of all this, I heard my name called. It was my turn to recite. What would I not give to be able to say that dreadful rule for the participle all through, very loud and clear, and without one mistake? But I got mixed up on the first words and stood there, holding on to my desk, my heart beating, and not daring to look up.

I heard M. Hamel say to me, "I won't scold you, little franz; you must feel bad enough. See how it is! Every day we have said to ourselves, 'Bah! I've plenty of time. I'll learn it tomorrow.' And now you see where we've come out. Ah, that's the great trouble with Alsace; she puts off learning till tomorrow. Now those fellows out there will have the right to say to you,'How is it; you pretend to be Frenchmen, and yet you can neither speak nor write your own language?'But you are not the worst, poor little Franz. We've all a great deal to reproach ourselves with."

(i) What was Franz thinking of when they called his name?
How did he want to perform his recitation?
How did he perform his recitation in reality? [Recall and Understanding] (3)

(ii) What was Franz feeling after his recitation? [Understanding] (3)

(iii) How did he expect M. Hamel to respond?
How did M. Hamel respond in reality? [Understanding] (3)

(iv) 'Now those fellows out there will have the right to say to you'
Who is referred to as 'those fellows'?
What would they say to them? [Recall and Understanding] (3)

(v) According to M. Hamel, what was the problem Alsace faced?
What was the consequence of this problem? [Analysis] (4)

Section D (Answer one or more questions from this Section)

POETRY

(Treasure Chest - A Collection of ICSE Short Stories and Poems)

SP-06

Question 6.

Read the following extract from H. W. Longfellow's poem 'Haunted Houses' and answer the questions that follow.

All houses wherein men have lived and died
Are haunted houses. Through the open doors
The harmless phantoms on the errands glide,
With feet that make no sound upon the floors.
We meet them at the door-way, on the stair,
Along the passages they come and go,
Impalpable impressions on the air,
A sense of something moving to and fro.
There are more guests at table than the hosts
Invited; the illuminated hall
Is thronged with quiet, inoffensive ghosts,
As silent as the pictures on the wall.

(i) Where can we 'meet' these 'phantoms' in the house? [Recall] (3)

(ii) What do the 'harmless phantoms' do through the doors? [Recall] (3)

(iii) Do the phantoms make any sound? [Recall] (3)

(iv) What does the poet mean by saying the ghosts 'throng' the hall? [Understanding] (3)

(v) Explain the line "As silent as the pictures on the wall". [Understanding] (4)

Question 7.

Read the following extract from Maya Angelou's poem 'When Great Trees Fall' and answer the questions that follow.

Great souls die and
our reality, bound to
them, takes leave of us.
Our souls,
dependent upon their
nurture,
now shrink, wizened.
Our minds, formed
and informed by their
radiance, fall away.
We are not so much maddened
as reduced to the unutterable ignorance of
dark, cold
caves.

(i) The poet refers to a new reality in the above extract. State the reason behind this new reality and what happens in it. [Evaluative] (3)

(ii) What do they mean by 'utterable ignorance'? [Recall] (3)

(iii) Who does 'nurture and radiance' affect?

How do they affect them? [Recall and Understanding] (3)

(iv) What happens to our souls and minds? [Recall and Understanding] (3)

(v) Explain how the loss of someone can lead to existential crisis in people. [Analysis] (4)

Answers *in Topper's Style*

1. (i) (c) Octavius was unsafe as he was the next heir to the throne.
   (ii) (b) Symbol of betrayal
   (iii) (d) insignificant
   (iv) (d) All of these
   (v) (a) swallowing hot coal
   (vi) (d) Messala
   (vii) (d) A pathway between Earth and spirit world
   (viii) (a) III, IV, I and II
   (ix) (c) Words unsaid
   (x) (c) Satire
   (xi) (c) Both (a) and (b)
   (xii) (a) I is true and II is false.
   (xiii) (d) Getting stuck in an elevator.
   (xiv) (c) Her granddaughter's legs.
   (xv) (d) People prefer television shows to books now.
   (xvi) (a) M. Hamel's patriotism

2. (i) Brutus is sitting inside his tent in Sardis. They have set up camp there before they march to Phillip for battle in the morning.

   Brutus sees the apparition of Caesar enter his tent.

   (ii) After seeing the monster-like spirit, Brutus is gripped with fear. His blood became cold and his hair stood up like when one gets goosebumps.

   The line 'That makes my blood cold and my hair to stare' ? from the extract explains Brutus feelings.

   (iii) Varro, Claudio and Lucious were also present in the above scene. However, they all were sleeping inside Brutus' tent.

   No, they neither see nor interact with Caesar's ghost.

   (iv) When Brutus saw the apparition, he was scared but demanded to know who it was. Caesar's spirit told him that it was Brutus evil spirit and that he would meet him again in Philippi.

   Brutus is shaken by the encounter with the spirit. When he gains back his courage, he awakens everyone and decides to march to Philippi immediately.

   (v) The phrase 'How ill this taper burns!' refers to the candle in Brutus tent whose flame suddenly starts to flicker and burn dimly. The day before the battle, everyone is asleep except Brutus. He has trouble falling asleep. It happens when the flame of the candle in his tent starts to flutter and burn weakly, creating a spooky and chilling atmosphere. Brutus is alarmed by the presence of an apparition in his tent. He questions the presence of the ghost by asking it 'Art thou any thing?' wondering if it might be a hallucination. He later, himself answers the question by inquiring its nature by asking if it is a god, an angel or a devil.

3. (i) 'He' in the above line refers to Julius Caesar.

   Antony is talking about him as Caesar was wronged and murdered by corrupt politicians.

   (ii) Antony is addressing the crowds at Caesar's funeral in above lines. He uses this opportunity to inform the plebeians of the injustice and betrayal Caesar had faced by the hands of the conspirators.

   (iii) In the above lines, Antony is conveying his agony to the crowd. He recollects the time when Caesar had been a loyal friend to the citizens. He tells them that Caesar cried for the poor. He had a special place in his heart for them.

   He shares his dilemma of how to consider such a soft man as 'ambitious'. He argues that ambitious people are cold-hearted and unemotional. He questions if the citizens could consider as sensitive as Caesar as 'ambitious' as Brutus calls him. Yes, his argument with several others is able to paint Caesar in a good light.

   (iv) Antony reminds the crowd that he had presented Caesar with the crown thrice. If Caesar wanted, he could have been the King of Rome. However, Caesar refused each time. He subtly argues that if Caesar was ambitious, he would have accepted the crown like any other ambitious man.

   (v) Antony belittles Brutus using his amazing oratory skills. He uses words like 'honourable' for Brutus and 'ambitious' for Caesar. But both are used ironically. He paints Caesar's 'ambition' as a tough decision Caesar made for the greater good of Rome. Simultaneously, he calls Brutus 'honourable' but diminishes Brutus credibility by making the crowd aware of Caesar's greatness and sacrifice.

   Caesar was a dear friend of Antony. As Brutus is one of the conspirators who plotted against Caesar, Antony is trying to inform people of his treachery and avenge his friend's death.

4. (i) Dogs were the only beings outside other than Mr. Mead.

He was wary of them as they would bark and make loud noises at the sound of hard heels hitting the pavement. So, instead, he wore his sneakers to avoid interaction with them.

(ii) The author compared 'the cottages and homes' with graveyards and only glimmering lights as a sign of existence. He compares the shadows of the people living in the houses with gray phantoms as an addition to the graveyard imagery.

(iii) Mr. Mead thought about the difference between the lives of his neighbours and him. He thought about the television shows and activities his neighbours are busy performing inside while he chooses to walk in the streets at night like a lonesome hawk in the mid-country. The barren streets remind him of plain, wind-less Arizona desert.

(iv) Mr. Mead was headed to the West towards the hidden sea that night.
On his way, he saw leaves on his way that he would usually step on or inspect them for their skeleton pattern.
He felt the frost in the winter air and the cold light going on and off.

(v) Mr. Mead's unusual ritual consisted of a walk in the night before he went to sleep. He enjoyed the crispness and freshness of the autumn air which had started to turn a bit chilly. He had been going for walks alone for the past eight to ten years. His house and windows were decorated with electric lights on the outside that he left on at night.

Other people, on the other hand, stayed outside during the day and inside their homes during nights. This was the new directive followed by the society in this technologically-regulated world. Families watched television after dark. The lights in their houses were either dim or switched off and their curtains drawn.

5. (i) Franz was thinking about the sudden announcement of M. Hamel leaving Alsace.
Franz wanted his recitation to be loud and clear, without making any mistakes.

However, he was unable to do so and mixed up the first few words. Embarrassed by his blunder, he stood frozen on his seat waiting for M. Hamel's reaction.

(ii) Franz was feeling embarrassed and ashamed. He wanted the recitation to be perfect but he messed up the very first few words. He felt regretful for getting distracted from his lessons and taking them for granted.

(iii) Franz expected M. Hamel to scold him for his mistake and probably even reprimand him with his ruler.

However, M. Hamel surprised him. He informed him that he wouldn't scold him today as he recognises the shame he must already be feeling for his mistake.

(iv) 'Those fellows' refer to the Germans and Prussian soldiers that had acquired Alsace.

M. Hamel remorsefully states that as people of Alsace took the French lessons for granted, they were not very fluent in it. He argues that now the new rule would have the right to question them for being Frenchmen if they don't know their own language well.

(v) According to M. Hamel, Alsace faced the problem of procrastination and disregard for the privilege and freedom that they had. He complains that everyone puts off learning for tomorrow. They had prioritised their own personal gains and agendas over education which was a bad judgment on their part.

And now, with Alsace occupied by Germans, it is too late as now their mother tongue would be stripped from them. As a consequence, they will not be able to preserve their language and heritage they had the privilege of receiving. They would not be able to practice French as they were not fluent in it. Their language, like their freedom, would be lost forever.

6. (i) We can meet the phantoms at doorways, on staircases, along the passages, around the table and even in the hall.

(ii) The phantoms glide silently through the open doors. They don't disturb anyone and keep busy with their errands.

(iii) No, they don't make any sound. They just glide through the doors. Their feet make no noise on the floor and they just float around without harming anyone.

(iv) At the dinner table, the poet observes the presence of the ghosts as uninvited guests. He notices that their presence increases the number of guests at the dinner party. They actually outnumber the living guests.

Thus, the poet uses the word 'throng' to showcase the presence of many ghosts who hang around the house, inoffensively and indifferent to the living.

(v) The line "As silent as the pictures on the wall ." uses a simile. The line presents the nature of the ghosts in the houses. The quiet and harmless ghosts are compared to pictures that hang on the walls of the corridor. These pictures are silent and still, and offer no interference in any living being's life like the ghosts that exist in these houses.

7. (i) The poet states that when we lose people of great importance in our life, we are forced to live in a new reality.
This new reality is devoid of the presence of our loved ones. We miss them and feel lost without their guidance.

(ii) 'Utterable ignorance' refers to 'indescribable unawareness'. When we experience the death of someone of great importance in our life, we are left in a state of unawareness. Our agony is indescribable and we feel numb and cold from within.

(iii) 'Nurture and radiance' is used to describe the guidance and wisdom that was imparted to us by our loved ones before their demise. This affects us, the recipient of our loved one's protection. The guidance and wisdom that our role models share with us affects our life in a positive way. They play a massive role in shaping our lives.
Their importance is so great that the absence of our loved one leaves us lost and gripped with despair.

(iv) According to the poet, after the death of great people, our souls that used to depend on the guidance of our loved one, feels shrunken. We feel smaller and insignificant than before. Our minds that were filled with the knowledge and wisdom given by the loved one, feels dull and lost far away.

(v) The poem talks about the importance of certain people and their influence in our lives. These 'great souls' can be our role models or relatives that we look up to. When they die, their absence has a massive impact on our lives. These people were our safe spaces and their demise has taken their protection away from us. It creates a new reality where the fear of the unknown engulfs us. Their memories plague our minds painfully and remind us of our regrets of words unsaid. We retreat to solitude and question our existence in this new reality without them. The depression and grief make us spiral into an existential crisis where we ponder about our life with and without them.

SQP Code : **PB-7/10** Series ***i*-Succeed 7-25/10** Roll No.

Sample Question Paper 07

Literature in English 10th (Code 01)

General Instructions

1. You will not be allowed to write during the first 15 minutes. This time is to be spent in reading the question paper.
2. The time given at the head of this paper is the time allowed for writing the answers.
3. The paper has four Sections.
4. Section A is compulsory - All questions in Section A must be answered.
5. You must attempt one question from each of the Sections B, C and D and one other question from any section of your choice.
6. The intended marks for questions or parts of questions are given in brackets [ ].

Time : 2 Hrs.

Max. Marks : 80

Section A (Attempt all questions from this Section)

Question 1.

Choose the correct answer to the question from the given options. (16)

(i) 'They fall their crests, and, like deceitful jades,
Sink in the trial. Comes his army on' ?
Who spoke the above lines and to whom? [Recall]

(a) Brutus to Cassius
(b) Brutus to Antony
(c) Antony to Brutus
(d) Cassius to Brutus

(ii) Before the battle at Philippi, Octavius disagrees with Antony's orders and insists that he .... [Recall]

(a) will go left instead of right
(b) will go right instead of left
(c) will go and attack before Antony's forces
(d) will go and attack after Antony's forces

(iii) 'The Sun of Rome is set'!

Who does Titinius call 'The Sun of Rome' in the above line? [Recall]

(a) Brutus
(b) Caesar
(c) Cassius
(d) Titinius

(iv) Who is Octavius? [Recall]

(a) Caesar's close friend
(b) Caesar's nephew
(c) Caesar's brother
(d) Caesar's adopted son

(v) 'A hot friend cooling: ever note, Lucilius,
When love begins to sicken and decay
It useth an enforced ceremony.'
Which word in the above lines means 'deterioration of conditions'? [Recall]

(a) Sicken (b) Useth (c) Decay (d) Enforced

(vi) Choose the option that lists the sequence of events from William Shakespeare's play *'Julius Caesar'* in the correct order. [Recall]

I. Brutus tells Cassius about his worries and that Portia killed herself by swallowing burning coal after discovering the news of Antony and Octavius joining forces against Brutus.

II. Cassius reminds Brutus that he cannot control him as Cassius is an older and more experienced soldier than him.

III. The ghost of Caesar tells Brutus that he will see him at Philippi and disappears.

IV. Cassius condemns Brutus for disapproval of Lucius Pella for accepting bribes, even after Cassius sent him a letter vouching for him.

(a) IV, II, III and I (b) IV, II, I and III
(c) II, IV, I and III (d) II, III, I and IV

(vii) Which of the following lines uses the same poetic device as 'a wind went with their paws'? [Understanding]

(a) Valour and love, and a king above, and the royal beasts below
(b) The leap was quick, return was quick
(c) And truly 'twas a gallant thing to see that crowing show
(d) Ramped and roared the lions, with horrid laughing jaws

(viii) In the poem 'When Great Trees Fall', which of the following options denotes that the impact of fallen trees is felt far and wide? [Recall]

(a) Might elephants lumber to safety. (b) Rock on distant hills shudders.
(c) Lions hunker down in tall grasess. (d) Mind escapes to the dark, cold caves.

(ix) In Robert Frost's poem 'A Considerable Speck', what does the poet disapprove of? [Recall]

(a) Collectivism (b) Powerful mind
(c) The mite (d) Rich people

SP-07

(x) According to H. W. Longfellow's poem 'Haunted Houses', which of the following is false about the phantoms? [Recall]

(a) They are offensive and dangerous for the living.
(b) They hold on to the deeds of the houses.
(c) They move around the house soundlessly.
(d) They run around doing errands of their own.

(xi) Which sentence below uses the correct meaning of the word 'sagacious'? [Understanding]

(a) The goat was provoked to attack Bhisma.
(b) The robbers were ruthless and didn't leave behind a single penny.
(c) The walls were coloured in a soothing sage green, to match the furniture.
(d) The wise men of the village made a collective decision.

(xii) In the short story 'With the Photographer', the photographer told the narrator that the face would be better .... [Recall]

(a) two-quarters full (b) One-fifth full
(c) three-quarters full (d) three-fifth full

(xiii) What did little Franz do instead of attending lessons in Alphonse Daudet's short story 'The Last Lesson'? [Recall]

(a) Visit his relatives
(b) Play outside with his friends
(c) Worked with his father at his shop
(d) None of these

(xiv) 'Where only the faintest glimmers of firefly light appeared in flickers behind the windows'

What does the underlined word imply about the lights presented in Ray Bradbury's short story 'The Pedestrian'? [Recall]

(a) The lights in the houses could be seen flickering before dimming out.
(b) The house was lit up with fireflies.
(c) The people were watching fireflies in the sky from behind the windows.
(d) The shadows of people glimmered faintly before disappearing.

(xv) In the short story 'The Elevator', what was 'like a nightmare' for Martin? [Recall]

(a) The fat lady with no chin and huge mass of neck.
(b) The woman was in the way and Martin could not escape the elevator.
(c) The fat lady knew which floor Martin lived on.
(d) The fat lady got on the elevator on the third floor, as if she knew Martin was there.

(xvi) Select the option that shows the correct relationship between Statements (I) and (II) from Ama Ata Aidoo's short story 'The Girl Who Can'. [Analysis]

Statement I Adjoa, despite having thin legs and weak legs, was selected to participate as an athlete in the state games.

Statement II Adjoa's Mother stood up to Nana when Adjoa was selected to compete at a race as an athlete. She made sure Nana gave Adjoa her approval to participate in the games.

(a) I is true and II is false .
(b) II is true and I is false.
(c) I and II are true.
(d) I and II are false.

Section B (Answer one or more questions from this Section)

DRAMA

Julius Caesar

By William Shakespeare

SP-07

Question 2.

Read the extract given below and answer the questions that follow.

Brutus : O Cassius, I am sick of many griefs.
Cassius : Of your philosophy you make no
use, If you give place to accidental evils.
Brutus : No man bears sorrow better. Portia is dead
Cassius : How 'scaped I killing when I cross'd you so?
O insupportable and touching loss! Upon what sickness?

(i) Where is this conversation taking place?
What was the state of mind of Cassius and Brutus before this conversation?
What is their current state of mind? [Recall and Understanding] (3)

(ii) What is the 'philosophy' Cassius is talking about?
Does Cassius agree with it? [Recall and Understanding] (3)

(iii) State two accusations Brutus talks about with Cassius.
How does Cassius respond to them? [Recall and Understanding] (3)

(iv) Who was Portia?
How deeply does her death affect Brutus? [Recall and Understanding] (3)

(v) What happens at the end of the scene?
How does Brutus react to it? [Recall and Understanding] (4)

Question 3.

Read the extract given below and answer the questions that follow.

Antony : This was the noblest Roman of them all;
All the conspirators save only he
Did that they did in envy of great Caesar;
He only, in a general honest thought
And common good to all, made one of them.

(i) Where is Antony in the above scene?
Who is he talking about and to whom? [Recall] (3)

(ii) What does 'noblest' mean?
Why does Antony use that word for Brutus? [Recall and Understanding] (3)

(iii) Antony uses the following words in his speech above for Brutus. Give an example from the play that justifies the use of these words for Brutus. [Recall] (3)

(a) Common good (b) Honest thought

(iv) What other things did Antony say about Brutus?
How did Octavius react to Antony's words? [Recall and Understanding] (3)

(v) How did Brutus die?
Why did he choose to die this way? [Understanding and Analysis] (4)

Section C (Answer one or more questions from this Section)

PROSE-SHORT STORIES

(Treasure Chest - A Collection of ICSE Short Stories and Poems)

Question 4.

Read the following extract from Stephen Leacock's short story 'With the Photographer' and answer the questions that follow.

I wanted something that my friends might keep after my death, to reconcile them to my loss. It seems that I was mistaken. What I wanted is no longer done. Go on, then, with your brutal work. Then when you have done all that-keep it for yourself and your friends. They may value it. To me it is but a worthless bauble." I broke into tears and left.

(i) Who is the narrator talking to?
Why does he want to get a picture of him? [Recall and Understanding] (3)

(ii) The narrator calls the photograph a 'worthless bauble'.
What does bauble mean?
Why did he say so? [Recall and Understanding] (3)

(iii) The narrator seems to get emotional at the end. Why? [Analysis] (3)

(iv) What were the narrator's expectations from the photographer?
Did he meet the narrator's expectations? [Recall and Understanding] (3)

(v) What are your thoughts about the photographer?
Do you have any suggestions for him? [Understanding and Analysis] (4)

Question 5.

Read the following extract from Ama Ata Aidoo's short story 'The Girl Who Can' and answer the questions that follow.

"........ That 'even though some legs don't have much meat on them, to carry hips.. they can run. Thin legs can run... then who knows?..." I don't know too much about such things. But that's how I was feeling and thinking all along. That surely, one should be able to do other things with legs as well as have them because they can support hips that make babies. Except that I was afraid of saying that sort of thing aloud. Because someone would have told me never, never but NEVER to repeat such words. Or else, they would have laughed so much at what I'd said, they would have cried.

It's much better this way. To have acted it out to show them, although I could not have planned it. As for my mother, she has been speechless as usual.

(i) What did Adjoa change Nana's perspective about?
How did she do so? [Recall and Understanding] (3)

(ii) Why was Nana worried about Adjoa initially?
Was her worry resolved? [Recall and Understanding] (3)

(iii) Why was Adjoa reluctant to tell everyone other uses of legs? [Analysis] (3)

(iv) 'She has been speechless as usual'
Who did Adjoa say this about?
Why? [Recall and Understanding] (3)

(v) Was Adjoa becoming an athlete a blessing in disguise?
Why? [Recall and Understanding] (4)

Section D (Answer one or more questions from this Section)

POETRY

(Treasure Chest - A Collection of ICSE Short Stories and Poems)

Question 6.

Read the following extract from Sukumar Ray's poem 'The power of Music' and answer the questions that follow.

But now there comes a billy goat, a most
sagacious fellow,
He downs his horns and charges straight, with
bellow answ'ring bellow.
The strains of song are tossed and whirled by
blast of brutal violence,
And Bhisma Lochan grants the world the golden
gift of silence.

(i) What did the billy goat do? [Recall] (3)

(ii) What adjectives are used for the goat and why? [Recall] (3)

(iii) What is the 'golden gift' in the above extract? [Recall] (3)

(iv) Do you think the villagers supported the goat's actions? Why? [Understanding and Analysis] (3)

(v) What was the overall theme of the poem? Explain it in brief. [Understanding and Analyssi] (4)

Question 7.

Read the following extract from Robert Frost's poem 'A Considerable Speck' and answer the questions that follow.

But this poor microscopic item now!
Since it was nothing I knew evil of
I let it lie there till I hope it slept.
I have a mind myself and recognise
Mind when I meet with it in any guise
No one can know how glad I am to find
On any sheet the least display of mind.

(i) What fate does the poet decide for the mite? [Recall] (3)

(ii) Why does the poet make that decision? [Analysis] (3)

(iii) The poet was glad about something. What was it? [Recall] (3)

(iv) Earlier in the poem, what does the poet say he doesn't like? [Recall] (3)

(v) What similarity does the poet think he and the mite have? What made the poet realise this similarity? [Recall and Understanding] (4)

Answers in Topper's Style

1. (i) (a) Brutus to Cassius
   (ii) (b) Will go right instead of left
   (iii) (c) Cassius
   (iv) (d) Caesar's adopted son
   (v) (c) Decay
   (vi) (b) IV, II, I and III
   (vii) (d) Ramped and roared the lions, with horrid laughing jaws
   (viii) (b) Rock on distant hills shudders.
   (ix) (a) Collectivism
   (x) (a) They are offensive and dangerous for the living.
   (xi) (d) The wise men of the village made a collective decision.
   (xii) (c) three-quarters full
   (xiii) (d) None of these
   (xiv) (a) The lights in the houses could be seen flickering before dimming out.
   (xv) (d) The fat lady got on the elevator on the third floor, as if she knew Martin was there.
   (xvi) (d) I and II are false.

2. (i) Brutus and Cassius are inside Brutus tent in Sardis.

   Before this conversation, Brutus and Cassius had an argument. They exchanged strong words where they accused each other of various things. Brutus accuses Cassius for taking bribes while Cassius accuses Brutus of slighting him by not supporting Pella even after he vouched for him.

   However, after their outbursts, they calm down a little. They express their regrets and importance of reconciliation in the current circumstances. They decide to become friends again.

   (ii) Cassius is talking about Brutus philosophy about being noble. When Brutus learns about Cassius accepting bribes, he criticises his actions. He argues that they are fighting for a noble cause and their actions should also be honourable.

   Cassius disagrees with Brutus. He calls him a hypocrite by not practicing his philosophy and giving way to chance misfortunes. He complains about Brutus ill-behaviour towards him.

   He accuses him of treating him like an enemy and a slave, disrespecting him by not trusting him and not overlooking his small mistakes.

   (iii) Brutus accuses Cassius of siphoning off money and cheating the people of their country. He also accuses him of refusing to send some of that money to pay their soldiers.

   Cassius is furious about Brutus allegations. In his anger, he takes out his dagger and asks Brutus to kill him with it.

   (iv) Portia was Brutus wife.

   Her death devastates Brutus. It plays some part in Brutus disturbed mood in the given scene. She was a true equal partner to Brutus. Whenever he felt troubled, she would boldly approach him to share his burden.

   She respected and valued her husband deeply. Brutus often felt that he was unworthy of someone as amazing as her. Her death deeply affected Brutus and had a damaging effect on his strength and courage.

   (v) At the end of the scene, Brutus has a frightening encounter with Caesar's ghost. After resolving his dispute with Cassius, they decide to meet their enemy halfway at Philippi for battle the next day. At night, everyone is asleep except Brutus who has trouble falling asleep. He is then visited by Caesar's ghost who warns Brutus that he would see him again at Philippi.

   Brutus is shaken by his experience. He wakes everyone up in his tent and decides to march to Philippi. He leaves a message for Cassius to follow him the next day with the troops.

3. (i) Antony is at the war field in Philippi in the above scene.

   He is talking about Brutus to Octavius.

   (ii) 'Noblest' means a person with high moral principles. They are righteous both of mind and heart.

   Antony uses the word 'noblest' for Brutus as he is the only conspirator that killed Caesar for his country. He didn't envy Caesar or his position and held any personal grudge against him. He participated in his assassination only for the welfare of Rome.

   (iii) (a) Brutus only reason to participate in the conspiracy against Caesar was that he truly believed that Caesar's death was in the best interest of Rome. He had no envy or personal grudge against him. He believed the common people would benefit with Caesar gone.

(b) Brutus was an honest man. He never shied away from accepting his faults. Even after Caesar's death, he never claimed direct power or tried to use his position to his own benefit. In fact, he condemns his close friend Cassius when he learns of his dishonesty.

(iv) Antony sang more praises of Brutus. He called him the noblest man in Rome. He said that even nature might stand up and declare Brutus worthiness.

Octavius agreed with Antony. He said that they should treat Brutus with honour and respect. He announced to bury him with the military honour that he deserved.

(v) Brutus committed suicide. At the battle of Philippi, he saw that his army was defeated and Cassius had committed suicide. Sensing the enemy is near, he asks Strato, his bondsman, to hold his sword as he runs into it. Brutus dies with Caesar's name on his lips.

Brutus wanted to keep his honour and dignity intact. He didn't want to die by the hands of the enemy. So, he decides to take his own life instead.

4. (i) The narrator is talking to the photographer.

He wants to get a picture of him clicked so that his loved ones have something to remember him by. He thought a photograph would be a good memento for them.

(ii) A bauble is a trinket or decoration. In informal language, a bauble can also mean a showy or worthless thing.

The narrator observes that the photographer had modified his features to such an extent that it was unrecognisable. The photographer's need to produce a 'perfect' photo with 'perfect' features, with no regards to the narrator's appearance, made the narrator feel disrespected. Hence, the narrator calls the photograph a 'worthless bauble'.

(iii) The narrator was emotional at the end of his experience with the photographer because he felt humiliated. The photographer's blunt and insensitive comments about his looks made the narrator feel self-conscious and miserable. After receiving severely edited photographs, the narrator's images were unidentifiable as their own.

(iv) The narrator expected to receive a photograph with their natural appearance from the photographer. He needed a good picture of himself as a reminder for his friends after his death.

The photographer didn't meet the narrator's expectations. During the picture taking session, the photographer bluntly commented negatively on the narrator's appearance. And the picture he produced in the end was highly altered and strayed very far from the narrator's natural features.

(v) In my opinion, the photographer is a very insensitive and superficial individual. He was foolish and unprofessional in his conduct towards the narrator. As a photographer, he has the tools to capture people in their rawest form. He has no right to make such insensitive comments about anyone's appearance. But, he still chose to obsess over his own ideas of perfection, hurting the narrator's sentiments in the process.

I would suggest the photographer to have a more professional and empathetic behaviour towards his customers and other people in general. He should refrain from voicing his insensitive opinions on someone's appearance and instead focus on delivering the kind of photographs his customers ask for.

5. (i) Adjoa changed Nana's perspective about the usability of her thin legs.

She participated in the district level games as a runner and won the competition. Nana was astonished and happy by her achievement. Her achievement challenged Nana's previous concerns and notions about her thin legs and helped change her perspective about them.

(ii) Nana was worried about Adjoa's legs. She believed Adjoa's legs were too thin and weak for a woman. She associated legs with a woman's childbearing capabilities and strongly believed that only women with strong and sturdy legs were capable of giving birth to strong babies.

Yes, her worries were later resolved when Adjoa won a race in the district games with her thin legs. This proved to Nana that her thin legs were strong enough.

(iii) Adjoa's Nana was a very strict woman. She was stubborn in her ideologies and beliefs. In the past, whenever she voiced her opinions in front of Nana or other old people in the village, she got ridiculed. Elders would either laugh at her ideas by not taking her seriously. They would scold and silence her when they disagreed with her views. The idea of getting brushed off again made her reluctant to tell everyone about the other uses of legs.

(iv) Adjoa said the above line about her mother, Kaya.

Throughout the short story, Adjoa mentions her mother being speechless in front of Nana. Her speechlessness is described as her usual behaviour as she is shown to be a calm and timid person. It also comes from being intimidated and overly judged by Nana who disapproves of Kaya's choice in a life partner and upbringing of Adjoa.

(v) Adjoa often felt unaccepted by Nana because of Nana's constant comments on her education and body. Nana's obsolete views about the world made her feel unheard and unappreciated. However, her becoming an athlete forced Nana to see her in a new light. Winning the race using her 'thin' legs that Nana had often thought of as weak was the greatest show of strength. It also displayed other important uses of a woman's legs other than child-bearing. It successfully broadened her mindset and made her appreciate Adjoa more. Her becoming an athlete was a blessing in disguise as it was the greatest argument Adjoa could have made to change Nana's narrow views.

6. (i) The billy goat attacked Bhisma Lochan by ramming him with his horns. Because of this, Bhisma Lochan stopped his forceful singing.

(ii) The adjective used for the goat in the poem is sagacious. It means wise. The goat is called wise as it was the only one who found a way to stop Bhisma from singing and teach him a lesson.

(iii) The 'golden gift' is the gift of silence Bhisma gives the people and animals around him. He stops singing after getting knocked down by the goat.

(iv) Yes, I think the villagers supported the goat's actions.

Bhisma was fond of singing and would sing loudly and continuously. His voice was so powerful and potent that it could be heard from miles. The loud nature of his voice made it difficult for the people around him to coexist with him. Even after several requests, Bhisma didn't listen and never stopped singing. But, after the goat knocks out Bhisma, he finally stops singing, liberating the villagers from his torment. Hence, the goat's actions were supported by the village.

(v) The poem is from the 'nonsense' genre where the poems are used to create fantasy stories. The poem talks about a fictional place where a person, Bhisma Kumar Lochan has agonised the village with his forceful singing. Even after many pleas, he doesn't stop. Eventually, the billy goat, who is world widely, rams Bhisma with his horns and teaches him a lesson. The lesson eventually break Bhisma's stubbornness and he stops his torture by turning silent for life.

7. (i) The poet decides to leave the mite alone. He also hopes that if he leaves the mite undisturbed, the mite might fall asleep.

(ii) The poet watches the mite smell or taste the drop of ink before deciding to run away from it. By observing the mite's behaviour, he deduces that it has a mind of its own. This impresses the poet as he didn't expect an insignificant microscopic creature to have that ability. Thus, he decides to leave the mite alone instead of killing it.

(iii) The poet was glad to find another creature that uses their minds before they act. The poet believes that many people even with privilege don't use their brains to their full capacity. So, he is glad to meet a creature who is small and insignificant but has the capacity to think and judge.

(iv) The poet mentions that he doesn't like people who are rich and privileged but dull and incapable of using their minds. He believes such people lack originality and creativity. He also expresses his disapproval of collectivism. He objects to mindless people exerting control over smart and underprivileged people to establish their superiority. He emphasised on the importance of individualism instead.

(v) The poet recognises that both he and the mite have a mind.

The poet realises their similarity based on the mite's action on the paper. After observing the poet near the paper, the mite tries to escape and save its life. In his hurry, the mite comes across the part of the sheet where the poet had dropped some extra ink drops while writing. Instead of running across it in panic, the mite stops and hesitantly inspects the ink drop first. Once he decides that the ink drop is harmful, the mite flies away from it in an instant.

This display of mind and deduction makes the poet realise their similarity.

SQP Code : **PB-8/10** Series ***i*-Succeed 8-25/10** Roll No.

Sample Question Paper 08

Literature in English 10th (Code 01)

General Instructions

1. You will not be allowed to write during the first 15 minutes. This time is to be spent in reading the question paper.
2. The time given at the head of this paper is the time allowed for writing the answers.
3. The paper has four Sections.
4. Section A is compulsory - All questions in Section A must be answered.
5. You must attempt one question from each of the Sections B, C and D and one other question from any section of your choice.
6. The intended marks for questions or parts of questions are given in brackets [ ].

Time : 2 Hrs.

Max. Marks : 80

Section A (Attempt all questions from this Section)

Question 1.

Choose the correct answer to the questions from the given options. (16)

(i) Antony wanted to see Caesar's will again. Why? [Understanding]

(a) To see how much Caesar owns.

(b) To reduce the amount of money left by Caesar to others.

(c) To calculate the amount left by Caesar to others.

(d) To keep all of Caesar's wealth for himself.

(ii) 'Our hearts you see not; they are pitiful;
And pity to the general wrong of Rome -'
Who is the 'general wrong of Rome'? [Recall]

(a) Julius Caesar (b) Mark Antony

(c) Decius Brutus (d) Marcus Brutus

(iii) Choose the option that lists the sequence of events from William Shakespeare's play *'Julius Caesar'* in the correct order. [Recall]

I. When plebeians come to know that Caesar left them some gardens and seventy-five drachmas each, they decide to cremate Caesar in a holy place and burn down the conspirator's houses.

II. Brutus clarifies to the crowd that Antony has no part in the conspiracy against Caesar but he will be a part of the new commonwealth.

III. Antony tells Octavius that Lepidus is fit to run errands but not to run one-third of the world.

IV. Cinna, the poet is accosted by the mob on the way to Caesar's funeral and they demand to know who he is and where he is going.

(a) II, III, I and IV
(b) I, IV, III and II
(c) I, IV, II and III
(d) II, I, IV and III

(iv) Titinius blamed Brutus for .... [Recall]

(a) allowing Cassius to take bribes
(b) letting his men run away from the battle
(c) letting Cassius commit suicide
(d) letting his army attack prematurely

(v) Why was the victory of Octavius and Antony described as 'vile'? [Understanding]

(a) As it would mean Caesar won.
(b) As it would mean Brutus and Cassius will become fugitives.
(c) As it would destroy democracy in Rome.
(d) None of the above

(vi) What is the Ides of March? [Recall]

(a) Fifteenth of March
(b) The day Julius Caesar dies
(c) A symbol of betrayal and downfall
(d) All of these

(vii) The tone of Sukumar Ray's poem 'The Power of Music' is .... [Understanding]

(a) frustrating
(b) vexed
(c) regretful
(d) comical

(viii) 'Our little lives are kept in equipoise

By opposite attractions and desires;'

What is the meaning of 'equipoise'? [Understanding]

(a) Equilibrium
(b) Parity
(c) Equity
(d) All of these

(ix) Select the option that shows the correct relationship between Statements (I) and (II) from Maya Angeleou's poem 'When Great Trees Fall'.

'The air around us becomes light, rare, sterile.' [Analysis]

Statement I The above line means that after a great loss of an important soul, the air around us becomes dull and drained of spirit.

Statement II The above line means that after a great loss of an important soul, the air around us becomes thin and is no longer richer or vibrant.

(a) I is true and II is false .
(b) II is true and I is false.
(c) I and II are true.
(d) I and II are false.

(x) 'With horrid laughing jaws'

What is the poetic device used in the above line from the poem 'The Glove and the Lions'? [Understanding]

(a) Alliteration
(b) Personification
(c) Simile
(d) None of these

(xi) 'I have a mind myself and recognise' means .... [Understanding]

(a) I have the capacity to make decisions
(b) I have the capacity to recognise things
(c) I have the capacity to mind my own business
(d) I have the capacity to write from my mind

(xii) In the short story 'The Pedestrian', why was Mr. Mead arrested? [Analysis]

(a) For robbing the bank
(b) For roaming the streets after dark
(c) For being different
(d) Both (b) and (c)

(xiii) The narrator was .... to see his picture, in the short story 'With the Photographer'. [Understanding]

(a) happy
(b) excited
(c) shocked
(d) scared

(xiv) In Alphonse Daudet's short story 'The Last Lesson', where were the villagers sitting in the classroom? [Recall]

(a) At the front of the classroom.
(b) On the back benches of the classroom.
(c) Outside the windows looking inside the classroom.
(d) They were not present in the classroom.

(xv) What advice did Martin's father give him in William Sleator's short story 'The Elevator'? [Recall]

(a) To grow up and shed all his fears
(b) To hit back his bullies at school
(c) To take the stairs as its good exercise
(d) To learn his participles on time

(xvi) Which of the following describe Nana the best from the short story 'The Girl Who Can'? [Understanding]

(a) Easy going
(b) Grumpy
(c) Timid
(d) None of these

Section B (Answer one or more questions from this Section)

DRAMA

Julius Caesar

By William Shakespeare

Question 2.

Read the extract given below and answer the questions that follow.

I am no orator, as Brutus is;
But, as you know me all, a plain blunt man,
That love my friend; and that they know full well
That gave me public leave to speak of him:
For I have neither wit, nor words, nor worth,
Action, nor utterance, nor the power of speech,
To stir men's blood; I only speak right on;
I tell you that which you yourselves do know;
Show you sweet Caesar's wounds, poor poor dumb mouths,
And bid them speak for me. But were I Brutus,
And Brutus Antony, there were an Antony
Would ruffle up your spirits, and put a tongue
In every wound of Caesar that should move
The stones of Rome to rise and mutiny.

(i) Who spoke the above lines?
Who is he addressing?
What is the occasion? [Recall and Understanding] (3)

(ii) What is he talking about in the above lines?
How does the crowd react after his speech? [Recall and Understanding] (3)

(iii) Antony uses verbal irony to provoke the crowd. How? [Understanding] (3)

(iv) But were I Brutus,
And Brutus Antony, there were an Antony
Would ruffle up your spirits, and put a tongue
In every wound of Caesar that should move
The stones of Rome to rise and mutiny.
Explain the meaning and significance of these lines. [Analysis] (3)

(v) Before this speech, Antony talks about Caesar's cloak.
Why does he mention it?
What role does it play in fulfilling Antony's motives? [Recall and Understanding] (4)

Question 3.

Read the extract given below and answer the questions that follow.

Octavius : You may do your will;
But he's a tried and valiant soldier.
Antony : So is my horse, Octavius; and for that
I do appoint him store of provender:
It is a creature that I teach to fight,
To wind, to stop, to run directly on,
His corporal motion govern'd by my spirit,
And, in some taste, is Lepidus but so;
He must be taught and trained, and bid go forth;
A barren-spirited fellow; one that feeds
On objects, orts, and imitations,
Which, out of use and staled by other men,
Begin his fashion: do not talk of him, But as a property.

(i) Who is Lepidus?
Why is Octavius defending him? [Recall and Understanding] (3)

(ii) Why does Antony not approve of Lepidus?
If he didn't approve of Lepidus, why did he agree to include him in the triumvirate? [Recall and Understanding] (3)

(iii) What does Antony compare Lepidus to? [Recall] (3)

(iv) After this conversation, Antony distracts Octavius from Lepidus' topic. How?
What are their plans going forward? [Recall and Understanding] (3)

(v) Which characteristics of Antony do we observe from this interaction?
Are they the same characteristics he displayed prior to this incident? [Recall and Understanding] (4)

Section C (Answer one or more questions from this Section)

PROSE-SHORT STORIES

(Treasure Chest - A Collection of ICSE Short Stories and Poems)

Question 4.

Read the following extract from Stephen Leacock's short story 'With the Photographer' and answer the questions that follow.

'Sit there, ' he said, 'and wait.'

I waited an hour. I read the Ladies Companion for 1912, the Girls Magazine for 1902 and the Infants Journal for 1888. I began to see that I had done an unwarrantable thing in breaking in on the privacy of this man's scientific pursuits with a face like mine.

After an hour the photographer opened the inner door.

'Come in,' he said severely.

I went into his studio.

'Sit down,' said the photographer.

I sat down in a beam of sunlight filtered through a sheet of factory cotton hung against a frosted skylight.

The photographer rolled a machine into the middle of the room and crawled into it from behind. He was only in it a second, - just time enough for one look at me, - and then he was out again, tearing at the cotton sheet and the window panes with a hooked stick, apparently frantic for light and air.

(i) Was the photographer busy when the narrator arrived?
How long did the narrator wait for him?
How did he pass his time when he was there? [Recall and Understanding] (3)

(ii) What did the narrator realise after reading the magazines?
What were the names of the magazines present in the room? [Recall] (3)

(iii) Describe the area the narrator was made to sit on when the photographer called him inside the studio. [Analysis] (3)

SP-08

(iv) What did the photographer do after asking the narrator to sit? [Recall] (3)

(v) How did the photographer react after observing the narrator through the machine?
What did he tell the narrator about his face? [Recall and Understanding] (4)

Question 5.

Read the following extract from Alphonse Daudet's short story 'The Last Lesson' and answer the questions that follow.

After the grammar, we had a lesson in writing. That day M. Hamel had new copies for us, written in a beautiful round hand: France, Alsace, France, Alsace. They looked like little flags floating everywhere in the school-room, hung from the rod at the top of our desks. You ought to have seen how every one set to work, and how quiet it was! The only sound was the scratching of the pens over the paper. Once some beetles flew in; but nobody paid any attention to them, not even the littlest ones, who worked right on tracing their fish-hooks, as if that was French, too. On the roof the pigeons cooed very low, and I thought to myself: 'Will they make them sing in German, even the pigeons?'

(i) What did the children study after grammar?
What did M. Hamel bring to class that day?
Why? [Recall and Understanding] (3)

(ii) What was distinctive about the copies handed out by M. Hamel? [Recall] (3)

(iii) How did the students react during the writing session?
Did anyone get distracted?
What about the littlest ones? [Recall and Understanding] (3)

(iv) What did Franz notice every time he looked up?
What was M. Hamel feeling during the class? [Recall] (3)

(v) Franz says 'Will they make them sing in German, even the pigeons'?
Why did he say so?
What does it mean? [Recall and Understanding] (4)

Section D (Answer one or more questions from this Section)

POETRY

(Treasure Chest - A Collection of ICSE Short Stories and Poems)

Question 6.

Read the following extract from Maya Angelou's poem 'When Great Trees Fall' and answer the questions that follow.

We breathe, briefly.
Our eyes, briefly,
see with
a hurtful clarity.
Our memory, suddenly sharpened,
examines,
gnaws on kind words
unsaid,
promised walks
never taken

(i) What do the eyes see 'briefly'? [Recall] (3)

(ii) How does the use of the word 'briefly' connect to our response while experiencing grief? [Understanding] (3)

(iii) What happens when we experience a moment of 'hurtful clarity'? [Understanding] (3)

(iv) What kind of words does our memory 'gnaws on'? [Recall] (3)

(v) "Promised walks never taken"
Why were the walks not taken?
What significance does it have in the poem? [Recall and Understanding] (4)

Question 7.

Read the following extract from H. W. Longfellow's poem 'Haunted Houses' and answer the questions that follow.

The spirit-world around this world of sense
Floats like an atmosphere, and everywhere
Wafts through these earthly mists and vapour dense
A vital breath of more ethereal air

(i) How supernatural and material worlds exist according to the extract? [Understanding] (3)

(ii) Which figure of speech is used in the above extract? [Understanding] (3)

(iii) How are the supernatural and material world connected to each other? [Understanding] (3)

(iv) Explain 'The spirit-world around this world of sense. Floats like an atmosphere' [Analysis] (3)

(v) How are human emotions affected by the spirit world? [Understanding] (4)

Answers *in Topper's Style*

1. (i) (b) To reduce the amount of money left by Caesar to others.

(ii) (a) Julius Caesar

(iii) (d) II, I, IV and III

(iv) (d) letting his army attack prematurely.

(v) (c) As it would destroy democracy in Rome.

(vi) (d) All of these

(vii) (d) comical

(viii) (d) All of these

(ix) (c) I and II are true.

(x) (b) Personification

(xi) (a) I have the capacity to make decisions

(xii) (d) Both (b) and (c)

(xiii) (c) shocked

(xiv) (b) On the back benches of the classroom

(xv) (a) To grow up and shed all his fears

(xvi) (d) None of these

2. (i) The above lines are spoken by Mark Antony.

He is addressing the plebians in Rome on the occasion of Caesar's funeral.

(ii) Antony is telling the crowd about the conspiracy against Caesar. He is praising Caesar for being a fair and noble ruler. He also sings praises of Brutus but he very clearly uses wordplay to discredit Brutus instead.

The crowd is enraged at the end of his speech. They feel cheated by Brutus and the other conspirators and remorseful on the death of their beloved Caesar. They vow to avenge Caesar's murder by killing the conspirators and burning their homes.

(iii) Antony presents himself to the crowd as a common person like them without power or worth. He claims he doesn't have the wit, words or skill to manipulate the crowd like Brutus who is a great orator. His comments, despite appearing to be in favour of Brutus, are actually against him. After his speech, the crowd realise that Brutus staged the entire event to justify the conspiracy against Caesar in his favour.

(iv) In the above lines, Antony states that, if he were in Brutus shoes or position of power, he would have used his influence and skills to exaggerate Caesar's wounds and provoke the crowd to rise up in rebellion. He would have argued that retaliation is the only way to such a scheme.

These lines played a significant role in painting Antony as a 'weakling' in front of the crowd. Using this card, Antony is able to gather public support and compassion towards Caesar's plight and at the same time, fuel hatred towards Brutus and other conspirators.

(v) Caesar's corpse is placed in a coffin and is wrapped in a blood-stained cloak.

Antony mentions this cloak to subtly remind people of Caesar's courage and demeanour. He claims that it was the same cloak he wore when he fought and won against the Nervii tribe in Belgium. The same cloak was now perforated with stabs made by conspirators like Cassius, Casca and Brutus and soaked in Caesar's blood.

The graphic display of Caesar's wounds and the disrespect of his cloak of honour makes the common people feel pity and grief towards Caesar. It drives them to mutiny and retaliation. This is what Antony wanted.

His motive was to use the cloak and other arguments to discredit Brutus and gain public favour and sympathy. He wanted people to rebel against the conspirators and help in his vengeance for Caesar's death.

3. (i) Lepidus is the third general that made the second triumvirate to rule the Roman empire with Octavius and Antony after the fall of Caesar.

Octavius is defending him as he believes that Lepidus is a tried and tested commander. He is the eldest out of the three that make up the triumvirate and holds the most experience and number of soldiers under his command.

(ii) Antony didn't view Lepidus as a significant or worthy man. His opinion about him was entirely opposite. He thought him to be talented enough to carry out routine everyday tasks. He didn't believe him to be as ambitious or bold as him and Octavius.

Despite his disapproval, he agreed to include Lepidus in the triumvirate as Lepidus had a large army that would be useful in their war against Brutus and Cassius. He would also shoulder the blame of any wrongdoings Antony or Octavius might conduct in the future.

(iii) Antony compares Lepidus to a horse as his value was the same as an animal that submits to its master. His loyalty motivates him to carry out his master's instructions. He also remarks that Lepidus is a superficial guy that adheres to old notions of fashion. He also compares him to a tool that can be employed or used when necessary. He considers him to be of low importance in a grand scheme of power relations.

(iv) Antony reminds Octavius to pay attention to more important things at hand to distract him from his conversation about Lepidus. He asserts that Brutus and Cassius had escaped and would undoubtedly be assembling their forces and preparing for a civil war. Thus, it was imperative for them to pool their resources and ensure their allies' support.

They plan to contact as many allies as possible to gain their support. They ought to prepare a strategy against the threat that was approaching them soon.

(v) A negative aspect of Antony's personality was revealed after Caesar's funeral. He ruthlessly orders to kill his political rivals including his own nephew. He has Lepidus fetch Caesar's will to manipulate and lessen the amount gifted by Caesar to the Roman populace. He even insults Lepidus behind his back by comparing him to a donkey or horse. He displays characteristics like arrogance and treachery by doing so. His cunningness and calculative nature is also displayed when he originally disapproves of Lepidus as the third ruler but later changes his mind just so he could use Lepidus as a figurehead for all his and Octavius crimes after the war.

Prior to this incident, he displayed qualities like loyalty, brotherhood and devotion towards his friend, Caesar. He bravely risks his life to prove Caesar's honour when Brutus tries to blacken it. So, the characteristics Antony displays before this incident is very different to what we see after the incident.

4. (i) The narrator doesn't know if the photographer was busy doing something but, when he arrived, the studio was empty with no other customers waiting.

The narrator waited an hour for the photographer. He passed his time by reading the few magazines present in the waiting room.

(ii) The narrator wondered if he had intruded on the photographer's scientific privacy by being there. The room had three magazines - Ladies Companion (1912), Girls Magazine (1902) and Infants Journal (1888).

(iii) The narrator was made to sit on a beam. The area was illuminated by a beam of sunlight that filtered through a sheet made up of factory cotton. The sheet was hung against a frosted window.

(iv) The photographer rolled the machine into the middle of the room and went behind it. He looked at the narrator through the machine and came out of it to adjust to the surroundings. He tore the cotton sheet from the window using a hooked stick as if he was frantic for more light and air in the room. Then, he went back behind the machine.

(v) The photographer looked very grave after observing the narrator through the machine. He was unhappy with how the narrator looked. According to him, the narrator didn't have ideal or beautiful features.

He told the narrator that his face looked quite wrong and would look better three-quarters full. He proceeded to nitpick everything that was wrong with the narrator's face and constantly instructed him to change it as much as possible.

5. (i) The children had a session of writing after grammar.

M. Hamel brought new copies for the class for their writing session.

He brought new copies as a parting gift for his students. After Germany's acquisition of Alsace, French was replaced by German as the official language. Thus, M. Hamel was leaving the school and the village the next day.

(ii) The copies were brand new and had 'France, Alsace, France, Alsace' written over them in a beautiful round hand. They looked like little flags passed around the school room, floating and hanging from the top of the desks of the students.

(iii) Everyone in the class focused on their writing. They set to work immediately. The room was very quiet and you could only hear the sound of scratching of pens on the paper.

No one got distracted from their task. Not even when some beetles flew inside the room.

The littlest ones were also absorbed with their work. They were concentrating on tracing their fish hooks as if it was French too.

(iv) Franz noticed M. Hamel sat still in his chair, gazing at everything around him one after the other. It looked like he was trying to memorise every little detail of his surroundings one last time.

M. Hamel was feeling lost and remorseful during the session. He loved his job and was devoted to his country and language. Losing the job that he had been doing for the past forty years was tough for him. He was feeling emotional and was trying to capture his surroundings in his mind one last time before leaving.

(v) Alsace and Lorriane, cities in France, were recently occupied by Germany with this, a new order to replace French with German language was passed. This change led to M. Hamel, the French teacher in a village of Alsace to leave the job he had dedicated forty years of his life to. With the new acquisition, Franz wondered if the Germans would now make the French pigeons sing in German too.

This line is another way of the author's way of emphasising Alsace's identity and freedom being in danger. Here the birds are a symbol of freedom as they can use their wings to fly anywhere in the world. Language, however, is a very crucial part of our expression and communication.

It is the means of conveying our ideas and thoughts freely. With Alsace's capture, their freedom and means of free expression was taken away from them. Thus, Franz wondering if the change of language will affect the birds as well is a reflection of Alsace's loss of freedom and autonomy.

6. (i) The given extract describes the eyes as going through a time of hurtful clarity, which suggests an abrupt, painful and vivid realisation of reality following a significant loss. It's a state in which we momentarily understand the reality of what is lost and that it is lost forever. It highlights regrets, unfulfilled intentions, spoken words of love and chances for shared experiences that will never come again.

(ii) The word 'briefly' is used in the poem to convey the transient nature of emotional moments that occur when we go through a significant loss. Briefly breathing and seeing suggests that the intense consciousness and clarity brought about by loss are fleeting yet razor-sharp. It implies that these fleeting yet profound moments of acute awareness and sorrow forces one to reflect deeply about the influence of the departed soul on our life.

(iii) When we experience a moment of 'hurtful clarity', our memory becomes more aware of the terrible truth of our loved ones passing. We remember the unsaid words and plans that we once expressed but can never fulfill anymore.

(iv) Our mind 'gnaws on' kind words could have been said by us to our loved ones but sadly weren't. We remember the instances where acts of kindness were withheld and pleasant words were unsaid, and our mind constantly stresses about it.

(v) The 'walks' were not taken as the significant person we intended to go on the walk with has died and is no longer with us.

The 'promised walks' represent the unfulfilled plans and shared experiences that were supposed to occur in our significant one's presence but it didn't. They also represent the wonderful and connecting moments that we shared with our loved ones before they departed. It plays a significant role in the poem as it brings attention to the feelings of regret and sadness that fill us after a great soul dies.

It signifies how influenced our life was by their presence and how much it would now change after they have departed.

7. (i) The extract presents the spirit world as a universal yet subtle presence that envelops the tangible, sensory world we live in. It draws a contrast between the supernatural and material realms. It implies that the spirit realm permeates the dense, physical reality like an invisible but necessary layer of atmosphere. The idea that the spirit world "wafts through these earthly mists and vapour dense" evokes a vision of a more elevated, refined existence that gives life to the physical realm.

(ii) A metaphor is the figure of speech used in the above extract.

Using this, the poet adds depth to the poem by implying that the spirit realm is mysterious and ever-present. The ethereal character of spirits interacts with the material world like the atmosphere that floats and wafts over earthy clouds. The metaphor also mentions the spiritual world as a source of 'vital breath,' underscoring its importance and providing support to the material world in a similar way to how air is to life.

(iii) The extract portrays a close-knit and intermingled link between the spirit-world and the corporeal world. The spirit-world encompasses the material world like an atmosphere implying that it is ever-present yet invisible. It illustrates how the spiritual realm is not distinct from the material world, but rather entwined with it, impacting and influencing it subtly. The relationship is further demonstrated by the idea that spirits go back to the locations they formerly called home. This suggests a continuous existence and link between the two worlds.

(iv) The above phrase emphasises widespread and constant presence of the spiritual world. Its presence is like the 'atmosphere' that we can 'feel' but not 'see' and is an essential component of our reality.

(v) The poem suggests a constant link between the material and the ethereal worlds by using the concept of a spirit realm connection with human emotions. The afterlife coexists with our physical world where memories and the presence of the deceased are sensed rather than seen.

It evokes strong feelings of melancholy and contemplation on the fleeting nature of our existence. The spirits influence our emotions by serving as a constant reminder of the legacies of our past lives rather than haunting us. It draws attention to the way that our experiences are entwined with our past, inspiring a deeper reflection on it. This leads to an emotional reflection on the afterlife and present life.

SQP Code : **PB-9/10**	Series ***i*-Succeed 9-25/10**	Roll No.					

Sample Question Paper 09

Literature in English 10th (Code 01)

General Instructions

1. You will not be allowed to write during the first 15 minutes. This time is to be spent in reading the question paper.
2. The time given at the head of this paper is the time allowed for writing the answers.
3. The paper has four sections.
4. Section A is compulsory - All questions in Section A must be answered.
5. You must attempt one question from each of the Sections B, C and D and one other question from any section of your choice.
6. The intended marks for questions or parts of questions are given in brackets [ ].

Time : 2 Hrs.

Max. Marks : 80

Section A (Attempt all questions from this Section)

Question 1.

Choose the correct answer to the questions from the given options. (16

(i) Cassius is not okay with Antony speaking at Caesar's funeral because .... [Analysis

(a) he thought Antony was Caesar's friend

(b) he thought Antony was a bad public speaker

(c) he thought Antony would lie to the crowd for his own cause

(d) he thought Antony would drive the crowd to mutiny

(ii) In Act IV Scene 1, The triumvirate was making a list of .... [Recall

(a) People they were going to kill

(b) Rules they were going to impose

(c) Commanders they were going to elect

(d) Allies they were going to approach

(iii) To showcase the dispute between Brutus and Cassius in Brutus tent before the battle of Philippi, which literary device is principally used? [Understanding

(a) Analogy

(b) Metaphor

(c) Irony

(d) Satire

(iv) What happened in Calpurnia's nightmare? [Recall

(a) Caesar was stabbed by Casca.

(b) Caesar's statue was broken by the Romans.

(c) Black crows surrounded Caesar.

(d) Caesar's statue was bleeding from multiple places.

(v) 'Thy life hath had some smatch of honour in it .'

What does the above line mean? [Understanding]

(a) Lucilius had always shown some honour in his life.
(b) Strato had always shown some honour in his life.
(c) Brutus had always shown some honour in his life.
(d) Cato had always shown some honour in his life.

(vi) What prediction of Antony about his enemy's strategy for the battle of Philippi that didn't come true? [Recall]

(a) Brutus and Cassius will send their armies first.
(b) The enemy will wait for them to initiate the attack.
(c) The enemy will not come down from the plains.
(d) Brutus and Cassius will try to attack them at night.

(vii) 'These perturbations, this perpetual jar
Of earthly wants and aspirations high,
Come from the influence of an unseen star
An undiscovered planet in our sky'

Which of the following words from the above extract means 'Never Ending or Changing' taken from 'The Haunted Houses' by HW Longfellow? [Understanding]

(a) Perpetual
(b) Undiscovered
(c) Perturbations
(d) Influence

(viii) Choose the option that lists the sequence of events from Maya Angelou's poem 'When Great Trees Fall' in the correct order. [Recall]

I. Our mind, impressed by the knowledge and the company of our loved one, now feels dull after their departure.
II. The air around us becomes light and flimsy. We are so overwhelmed with the loss of a significant person that we find it hard to breathe.
III. Time has allowed us to heal and we are filled with soothing electric vibrations. The pain and agony we once felt still buzzes within us but we continue to heal from the aftermath.
IV. When tall trees in the forest fall, the impact is felt far and wide. Even the rocks on the distant hill shake and rumble.

(a) IV, II, I and III
(b) IV, I, III and II
(c) IV, I, II and III
(d) IV, III, I and II

(ix) Which of the following animal lines themselves along the roadside in the poem 'The Power of Music'? [Recall]

(a) Goats
(b) Fishes
(c) Bulls
(d) Horses

(x) Which of the following themes does Leigh Hunt's poem 'The Glove and the Lions' not explore? [Understanding]

(a) Chivalry
(b) Vanity
(c) Pride
(d) Betrayal

(xi) What was the colour of Robert Frost's manuscript in 'A Considerable Speck'? [Recall]

(a) Grey
(b) Ivory
(c) White
(d) Light Brown

(xii) What were the advantages of having crutches according to Martin in the short story 'The Elevator'? [Understanding]

(a) He could stay home for sometime.

(b) His father will be more attentive to him.

(c) He could use the crutches to take the stairs.

(d) He didn't have to go to school and face his bullies.

(xiii) In Ama Ata Aidoo's short story 'The Girl Who Can', whenever Adjoa's Nana talked about her father, ... [Recall]

(a) Kaya would become very quiet

(b) the conversation would shift focus from her legs

(c) Adjoa felt angry and disappointed

(d) Adjoa's mother would become defensive and argue with her

(xiv) The mention of .... in the beginning of the short story 'The Last Lesson' indicates the state of war in Alsace. [Recall]

(a) Prussian soldiers

(b) Birds chirping in the woods

(c) Crowd in from of bulletin board

(d) M. Hamel leaving

(xv) 'This one particular house had all of its electric lights brightly lit, every window a loud yellow illumination, square and warm in the cool darkness'. [Understanding]

What does the lighting of Mr. Mead's house represented in the short story 'The Pedestrian'?

(a) Mr. Mead's obsession with Christmas lights.

(b) The activeness of Mr. Mead's mind.

(c) The contrast from the metallic coldness in the police car.

(d) All of the above

(xvi) Select the option that shows the correct relationship between Statements (I) and (II) from Stephen Leacock's short story 'With the Photographer'. [Recall]

Statement I The narrator was bitter as the photographer insulted his looks and changed his features according to the photographer's standard of good looks.

Statement II The photographer used photographic techniques like Delphide to change the narrator's look in the final photo.

SP-09

(a) I is true and II is true.

(b) II is true and I is false.

(c) II is the cause for I.

(d) I and II are independent of each other.

Section B (Answer one or more questions from this Section)

DRAMA

Julius Caesar

By William Shakespeare

Question 2.

Read the extract given below and answer the questions that follow.

Brutus : "All this!" ay, more: fret till your proud heart break;
Go show your slaves how choleric you are,
And make your bindmen tremble. Must I budge?
Must I observe you? Must I stand and crouch

Under your testy humour? By the gods,
You shall digest the venom of your spleen,
Though it do split you; for, from this day forth,
I'll use you for my mirth, yea, for my laughter,
When you are waspish.

Cassius : Is it come to this?

Brutus : You say you are a better soldier:
Let it appear so; make your vaunting true,
And it shall please me well: for mine own part,
I shall be glad to learn of abler men.

Cassius : You wrong me every way, you wrong me, Brutus;
I said, an elder soldier, not a better:
Did I say 'better'?

(i) Why was Cassius angry?
How did Brutus respond to his anger? [Analysis and Understanding] (3)

(ii) How did Cassius react to Brutus response?
What did he say to Brutus? [Recall and Understanding] (3)

(iii) Why were Cassius and Brutus arguing in the first place? [Understanding] (3)

(iv) State the meaning of the following words. [Understanding] (3)
(a) Choleric (b) Bondmen (c) Waspish

(v) Brutus calls Cassius a 'slightman'. Why? [Recall and Understanding] (4)
Was he justified?

Question 3.

Read the extract given below and answer the questions that follow.

Lucilius : Safe, Antony; Brutus is safe enough:
I dare assure thee that no enemy
Shall ever take alive the noble Brutus:
The gods defend him from so great a shame!
When you do find him, or alive or dead,
He will be found like Brutus, like himself.

Antony : This is not Brutus, friend, but I assure you,
A prize no less in worth: keep this man safe;
Give him all kindness: I had rather have
Such men my friends than enemies.
Go on,
And see whether Brutus be alive or dead;
And bring us word unto Octavius' tent
How every thing is chanc'd.

SP-09

(i) What did Lucilius say about Brutus?

Do they turn predictive? **[Recall] (3)**

(ii) Explain Lucilius character traits in these lines? **[Analysis] (3)**

(iii) What impression does Lucilius want to leave on Antony?

Was he successful? **(Recall and Understanding) (3)**

(iv) How does Antony react to Lucilius words?

How does Antony treat Lucilius? **(Recall and Understanding) (3)**

(v) Where is the above scene taking place?

Where is Brutus?

What happens to him after he learns of Antony's arrival? **(Recall and Understanding) (4)**

Section C (Answer one or more questions from this Section)

PROSE-SHORT STORIES

(Treasure Chest-A Collection of ICSE Short Stories and Poems)

Question 4.

Read the following extract from william sleator's short story 'The Elevator' and answer the questions that follow.

Martin started running down the stairs. The stairs were dark and he fell. His father was silent on the way to the hospital, disappointed and angry with him for being a coward and a fool. Martin had broken his leg and needed to walk on crutches. He could not use the stairs now. Was that why the fat lady had smiled? Did she know what would happen?

At least his father was with him in the elevator on the way back from the hospital. There was no room for the fat lady to get in, and if she did, his father would see her and maybe he would understand. When he got home, he could stay in the apartment for a few days. The doctor said that he had to rest as much as possible. Martin felt quite safe from the fat lady now.

"Oh, I almost forgot," his father reached out and pressed number nine.

"What are you doing?" asked Martin, trying not to sound afraid.

"I promised to visit Mrs. Ullamn," said his father, looking at his watch as he stepped out of the elevator.

(i) Why was Martin's father disappointed in him?

What was his general attitude towards Martin? **[Understanding and Analysis] (3)**

(ii) Why was Martin running down the stairs? **[Understanding] (3)**

(iii) Describe the staircase Martin was using. **[Understanding] (3)**

(iv) Who is Mrs. Ullman? Why is she important to the story? **[Recall and Understanding] (3)**

(v) Do you think Martin's fears were irrational? How do you think he could have overcome them?

[Recall and Understanding] (4)

Question 5.

Read the following extract from Ama Ata Aidoo's short story 'The Girl Who Can' and answer the questions that follow.

As far as I could see, there was only one problem. And it had nothing to do with what I knew Nana considered 'problems', or what Maami thinks of as 'the problem'. Maami is my mother. Nana is my mother's mother. And they say I am seven years old. And my problem is that at this seven years of age, there are things I can think in my head, but which maybe, I do not have proper language to speak them out with. And that, I think, is a very serious problem because it is always to decide whether to keep quiet and not say any of the things that come into my head, or say them and get laughed at. Not that it is easy to get any to listen to you, even when you decide to take the risk and say something serious to them.

(i) Who is 'I'?

Who are Nana and Maami?

Where do they all live? [Recall and Understanding] (3)

(ii) What are the 'problems' referred to in the extract? [Recall] (3)

(iii) How did Nana react whenever 'I' expressed her opinions? [Understanding] (3)

(iv) How did 'I' feel about Nana's reaction?

What did she start to do as a result? [Recall and Understanding] (3)

(v) What does Nana represent in the story? Explain with examples. [Evaluative and Analysis] (4)

Section D (Answer one or more questions from this Section)

POETRY

(Treasure Chest - A Collection of ICSE Short Stories and Poems)

Question 6.

Read the following extract from Leigh Hunt's poem 'The Glove and the Lions' and answer the questions that follow.

And truly 'twas a gallant thing to see that crowning show,
Valour and love, and a king above, and the royal beasts below.
Ramped and roared the lions, with horrid laughing jaws;
They bit, they glared, gave blows like beams, a wind went with their paws;
With wallowing might and stifled roar they rolled on one another;
Till all the pit with sand and mane was in a thunderous smother;
The bloody foam above the bars came whisking through the air;
Said Francis then, "Faith, gentlemen, we're better here than there".

(i) What is the 'gallant thing'? [Recall] (3)

(ii) Give any two examples from the text that uses alliteration as a poetic device. [Understanding] (3)

(iii) Describe the lion fight. [Understanding] (3)

(iv) Describe the ambience in the stadium during the lion fight. [Understanding] (3)

(v) What kind of environment has the poet created in the poem? How? [Recall and Understanding] (4)

Question 7.

Read the following extract from Robert Frost's poem 'A Considerable Speck' and answer the questions that follow.

A speck that would have been beneath my sight
On any but a paper sheet so white
Set off across what I had written there.
And I had idly poised my pen in air
To stop it with a period of ink
When something strange about it made me think,
This was no dust speck by my breathing blown,
But unmistakably a living mite
With inclinations it could call its own.

(i) What unusual thing does the poet see on his manuscript? **[Recall] (3)**

(ii) What was the poet doing when he saw the speck? **[Recall] (3)**

(iii) Describe the mite that the poet sees. **[Understanding] (3)**

(iv) How does the poet react to seeing the speck? **[Understanding] (3)**

(v) Analyse and explain the theme of the poem. Discuss poet's views about the significance of small forms of life. **[Analysis] (4)**

For Answers Scan QR Code

SQP Code : **PB-10/10**

Series *i*-**Succeed 10-25/10**

Roll No.

Sample Question Paper 10

Literature in English 10th (Code 01)

General Instructions

1. You will not be allowed to write during the first 15 minutes. This time is to be spent in reading the question paper.
2. The time given at the head of this paper is the time allowed for writing the answers.
3. The paper has four Sections.
4. Section A is compulsory - All questions in Section A must be answered.
5. You must attempt one question from each of the Sections B, C and D and one other question from any section of your choice.
6. The intended marks for questions or parts of questions are given in brackets [ ].

Time : 2 Hrs.

Max. Marks : 80

Section A (Attempt all questions from this Section)

Question 1

Choose the correct answer to the questions from the given options. (16)

(i) Who kisses Caesar's hand to support Metellus' request? [Recall]

(a) Brutus (b) Decius Brutus (c) Cinna (d) Metellus Cimber

(ii) What instruction does Brutus give Claudius and Varro after he wakes them up? [Recall]

(a) To inform Cassius to start off his forces early.

(b) To stay awake and guard him, as he was scared.

(c) To defend him from a ghost

(d) To punish Lucius for sleeping.

(iii) What is the irony in Brutus borrowing money from Cassius? [Understanding]

(a) He is richer than Cassius.

(b) They were fighting with each other recently.

(c) Brutus talks about integrity but is willing to accept money earned through deceit.

(d) Cassius was known to be a miser.

(iv) Why was Cinna, the poet, hesitant to walk around outside? [Understanding]

(a) The police were executing poor people.

(b) There is a fierce storm.

(c) People were angry at poets.

(d) The people were rioting over Caesar's assassination.

(v) 'You say you are a better soldier:
Let it appear so; make your vaunting true,
And it shall please me well: for mine own part,
I shall be glad to learn of noble men'.
The underlined word in the given extract means .... [Understanding]

(a) speaking aimlessly (b) speaking boastfully
(c) speaking illogically (d) speaking animatedly

(vi) What is Cassius reaction on seeing the standard bearer running with the flag? [Recall]

(a) He stopped him.
(b) He killed him and took the flag from him.
(c) He asked him to keep it somewhere safe.
(d) He took the flag and gave it to another soldier to carry.

(vii) The people requested Bhisma Lochan Sharma to stop singing in Sukumar Ray's poem 'The Power of Music' because .... [Understanding]

(a) they found his singing irritating
(b) they felt it was too loud to bear
(c) they thought his singing would kill them
(d) they wanted to make his singing pleasant

(viii) In Robert Frost's poem 'A Considerable Speck', what did the mite symbolise? [Understanding]

(a) The amazing world of microscopic creatures.
(b) Man's dominance over all the species.
(c) The capacity to think.
(d) The inferiority of tiny organisms

(ix) What figure of speech is demonstrated in the line "The struggle of the instinct that enjoys, And the more noble instinct that aspires" from the poem 'Haunted Houses'? [Understanding]

(a) Antithesis (b) Oxymoron
(c) Assonance (d) Simile

SP-10

(x) What is the humorous comment King Francis makes in the poem 'The Glove and the Lions'? [Recall]

(a) He said that the lions were not braver and more ferocious than him.
(b) He said that the king and others were better in their places than in the arena.
(c) He said he would reward the person who would jump in the arena.
(d) He said that the person who brings the Lady's glove back would be the bravest of all.

(xi) In Maya Angelou's poem 'When Great Trees Fall', what happens to the lions when great trees fall? [Recall]

(a) Lions remain unaffected (b) Lions move around it safely
(c) Lions stay down in tall grasses (d) Lions start to tremble

(xii) What is the importance of 'legs' in the story 'The Girl Who Can'? [Understanding]

(a) They help break Nana's myth about women.
(b) They help Adjoa get selected in district games.
(c) Nana realises that legs can be useful in so many ways.
(d) All of the above

(xiii) Why was Franz afraid of a scolding at school? [Analysis]

(a) He had bullied another boy.
(b) He knew nothing about participles.
(c) He was late to class.
(d) He had made fun of a teacher.

(xiv) What is the central point of the story 'With the Photographer'? [Recall]

(a) Acceptance
(b) Reality
(c) Confidence
(d) All of these

(xv) What could have saved Mr. Mead from being taken away by the police car? [Understanding]

(a) A little more argument
(b) Running away
(c) Shouting and gathering people
(d) A wife who could have provided an alibi for him

(xiv) Martin was scared of the old lady because [Understanding]

(a) she was very loud.
(b) she constantly stared at him.
(c) she had piggy eyes.
(d) Both (b) and (c)

Section B (Answer one or more questions from this Section)

DRAMA

Julius Caesar

By William Shakespeare

Question 2.

Read the extract given below and answer the questions that follow.

Brutus : Are yet two Romans living such as these?
The last of all the Romans, fare thee well!
It is impossible that ever Rome
Should breed thy fellow. Friends, I owe more tears
To this dead man than you shall see me pay.

(i) When is this dialogue taking place? Where is Brutus speaking this? [Recall and Understanding] (3)

(ii) What does Brutus say about his two friends that are lying dead? [Recall] (3)

(iii) Explain 'To this dead man than you shall see me pay.' [Analysis] (3)

(iv) 'The last of all the Romans'. Elaborate. [Analysis] (3)

(v) What traits does Brutus reveal by these lines?

Does Brutus appear to be a practical man in the above extract? [Recall and Understanding] (4)

Question 3.

Read the extract given below and answer the questions that follow.

If then that friend demand
why Brutus rose against Caesar, this is my answer:
– Not that I loved Caesar less, but that I loved
Rome more. Had you rather Caesar were living and die
all slaves, than that Caesar were dead, to live all free men?

(i) Who is the speaker of the above lines? What is he trying to convey through the opening lines of the speech? [Recall and Understanding] (3)

(ii) How does he soothe the doubt of people who considered Caesar a friend? [Understanding] (3)

(iii) 'Had you rather Caesar were living, and die
All slaves, than that Caesar were dead, to live all free men''?
What is the speaker trying to convey through these lines? [Recall] (3)

(iv) How does the speaker convince the crowd that Caesar's death was justified? [Understanding] (3)

(v) Does the speaker succeed in his attempt to justify the assassination?
What is the Crowd's reaction? [Recall and Understanding] (4)

Section C (Answer one or more questions from this Section)

PROSE-SHORT STORIES

(Treasure Chest : A Collection of ICSE Short Stories and Poems)

Question 4.

Read the following extract from William Sleator's short story 'The Elevator' and answer the questions that follow.

Martin didn't want to cry in front of his father, so he waited until he got to his room. His father probably knew he was crying anyway. He slept very little.

In the morning, when the elevator door opened, the fat lady was waiting for him. Martin stood there, unable to move, then backed away. As she saw him, her expression changed. She smiled as the door slammed.

Martin started running down the stairs. The stairs were dark and he fell. His father was silent on the way to hospital, disappointed and angry with him for being a coward and a fool. Martin had broken his leg and needed to walk on crutches. He could not use the stairs now. Was that why the fat lady had smiled? Did she know what would happen?

(i) What is the theme of the story 'The Elevator'? [Recall and Understanding] (3)

(ii) Why did Martin find the stairs bad and fearful like the elevator? [Recall and Understanding] (3)

(iii) How did Martin fracture his leg? [Understanding] (3)

(iv) Why did Martin's father scold him? [Analysis] (3)

(v) What happened one morning on the fourteenth floor? What was Martin's reaction? [Recall and Understanding] (4)

Question 5.

Read the following extract from Ray Bradbury's short story 'The Pedestrian' and answer the questions that follow.

A metallic voice called to him:
"Stand still. Stay where you are! Don't move!"

He halted.

"Put up your hands!"

"But-" he said.

"Your hands up! Or we'll Shoot!"

The police, of course, but what a rare, incredible thing; in a city of three million, there was only one police car left, wasn't that correct? Ever since a year ago, 2052, the election year, the force had been cut down from three cars to one. Crime was ebbing; there was no need now for the police, save for this one lone car wandering and wandering the empty streets.

(i) Who stopped Mr. Mead one day when he was on his usual evening walk? Why? [Recall and Understanding] (3)

(ii) How did the police speak to him? [Understanding] (3)

(iii) Why was Mr. Mead surprised? [Analysis] (3)

(iv) Why was the number of cars reduced from three to one? [Understanding] (3)

(v) Why did Mr. Mead look suspicious to the police car? [Analysis] (4)

Section D (Answer one or more questions from this Section)

POETRY

(Treasure Chest - A Collection of ICSE Short Stories and Poems)

Question 6.

Read the following extract from Maya Angelou's poem 'When Great Trees Fall' and answer the questions that follow.

When great trees fall,
rocks on distant hills shudder,
lions hunker down
in tall grasses,
and even elephants
lumber after safety.

(i) How does the imagery in the poem contribute to the overall theme of the poem? [Recall and Understanding] (3)

(ii) How does falling trees impact the animals? [Understanding] (3)

(iii) Explain how the above lines draw parallels between the reaction of nature and human beings when they experience profound changes. [Evaluative and Understanding] (3)

(iv) How does the loss of someone affect the people? [Understanding] (3)

(v) How does the image of rocks correlate with the fall of great trees? How does it make the base of the remaining poem? [Understanding and Analysis] (4)

Question 7.

Read the following extract from Sukumar Ray's poem 'The Power of Music' and answer the questions that follow.

When summer comes, we hear the hums
Bhisma Lochan Sharma.
You catch his strain on hill and plain from Delhi
down to Burma
He sings as though he's staked his life, he sings
as though he's hell-bent;
The people, dazed, retire amazed although they
know it's well-meant.
They're trampled in the panic rout or languish
pale and sickly,
And plead, "My friend, we're near our end, oh
stop your singing quickly!"

(i) Describe the extent of Bhisma Lochan Sharma's influence during the summer season? [Understanding] (3)

(ii) How did Bhisma Lochan Sharma sing? [Understanding] (3)

(iii) How did people react to his singing? [Understanding] (3)

(iv) Explain the line 'They're trampled in the panic rout or languish pale and sickly'. [Analysis] (3)

(v) Who was pleading and why? [Recall and Understanding] (4)

For Answers Scan QR Code

SP-10

Knowledge Booster Zone

Welcome to the Knowledge Booster Zone !

This section is dedicated to enhancing your understanding of key ideas associated with the stories poems and parts of the play.
Here, you will find chapter-wise revision notes designed to solidify your **foundational knowledge**. Use these notes to review and reinforce what you've learned, ensuring you're well-prepared to answer the questions.

Progress Tracker Tick the chapters as you revise them.

Prose

- [ ] With the Photographer
- [ ] The Girl Who Can
- [ ] The Last Lesson
- [ ] The Elevator
- [ ] The Pedestrian

Poetry

- [ ] Haunted Houses
- [ ] When Great Trees fall
- [ ] The Power of Music
- [ ] The Glove and the Lions
- [ ] A Considerable Speck

Drama

Julius Caesar

- [ ] Act III
- [ ] Act IV
- [ ] Act V

Prose

Chapter 1 With the Photographer

Author: Stephen Leacock

Setting

The story 'With the Photographer' is taken from Stephen Leacock's 'Behind the Beyond and other Contribution to Human Knowledge'. It unfolds in an old-fashioned studio lacking any modern equipment.

Main Characters

The narrator wanted to get his picture clicked.

The photographer a drooping man wearing a grey suit

Theme

The story conveys the theme of original self and distorted self. It also gives a message of acceptance and confidence.

Summary of the Chapter

- The story highlights the author's bitter experience with a photographer.
- The narrator went to the photographer to get his picture clicked. He wanted a memory for his friends and loved ones to remember him by, after he dies.
- The photographer was a drooping man wearing a gray suit. He looked unenthusiastic and detached like a scientist. He makes the narrator wait for an hour.
- The photographer's waiting room had magazines like Ladies Companion (1912), Girls Magazine (1902) and Infants Journal (1888). The narrator remarks that he didn't intend on disturbing the photographer while exploring his 'scientific' interest.
- Inside the photographer's studio, the narrator sits on the beam of sunlight, pouring through a frosted skylight which has a cotton cloth over it.
- The photographer rolled in the camera machine and looked at the narrator through it.
- The photographer is unsatisfied by the narrator's looks. He makes multiple comments like his face would look better three-quarters full, to open and close his mouth, his head and ears are bad, and so on.
- The narrator patiently listens to the photographer's critics. He is disheartened by his remarks but cooperates with him by following his instructions.
- Eventually, the narrator gets overwhelmed and snaps angrily at the photographer. He informs him that he is aware of not being a beauty but has come to accept his features as they are.
- The photographer is disinterested in the narrator's outburst and snaps the image while the narrator is speaking. He refuses to show the image he had captured and insists on showing the negative on Saturday.
- On Saturday, the narrator visits the photographer, who looks more intense and quiet than before. But he also appears to be proud of his work.
- The narrator is shocked to see that the picture had very little resemblance of him.
- The photographer, without the narrator's permission, chooses to alter the narrator's eyebrows, hairline, eyes, forehead and mouth using the Delphide method to fit his own idea of perfection.
- Only the narrator's ears are left untouched which the photographer plans to change using the new Sulphide method.
- The narrator is frustrated by the photographer's insensitivity. He screams at the photographer reminding him that he was unsuccessful in delivering results. He wanted the image of himself with the features as god gave him and not the distorted version that the photographer had produced.
- The narrator compares the altered image to a 'worthless bauble'. With his self-confidence shaken, he cries due to the humiliation and walks away.

- *Through the story, the author explores the theme of insecurity due to appearence. The magazines as well as the photographer have set standard of beauty which does not resemble the narrator.*
- *The narrator also seems to lack confidence to stand up for himself but gradually develops his self-worth.*

Values Imparted

- The story conveys the idea that ones physical appearance is a unique gift that should be accepted as it is without using artificial changes or 'improving' it.

Chapter 2 The Elevator

Author: William Sleator

Setting

The story 'The Elevator' is set in a small elevator in a small building.

Main Characters

Martin a 12 year old boy who is afraid of the old, rickety elevator in his building.

Martin's father thinks that his son is a coward and weak.

A fat lady stares at Martin, smiles creepily at him and scares him. She completely fills the elevator.

Theme

The story deals with the theme of fear and the importance of relying on one's knowledge and training in times of crisis.

Summary of the Chapter

- *The Elevator is a short about a twelve year old boy named Martin who has many fears like of his father of cramped spaces, etc.*
- *Martin moves into an old apartment building with his father which had a very small elevator with poor lighting, dirty walls and doors that closed too fast with a three person limit.*
- *The stairs were not a good alternative. It was dark with no windows and broken lights. Martin's footsteps echoed on the cement stairs which gave him an impression of being followed.*
- *When he used the stairs one day to reach his apartment on the seventeenth floor, he was out of breath and his father scolded him for not using the elevator. He often berated Martin for being skinny, weak and unathletic. To not disappoint his father further, Martin decides to take the elevator from that day. He wishes he would get used to it as he got used to being bullied at school. But he struggled to get over his fear.*
- *One morning, on his way to school, the elevator stopped at the fourteenth floor and a fat lady got in with Martin. She was very large with fleshy cheeks, blue piggy eyes, no chin and was wearing a old green coat. Her constant staring and loud breathing made Martin uncomfortable.*
- *On his way back from school, Martin wished he would be alone but the fat lady joined him in the elevator on the third floor. When the elevator stopped on Martin's floor, he had to squeeze around her to get off the elevator.*
- *Martin asked his father about the strange fat lady. His father, instead of showing concern, rebuked him for being too timid and cowardly. Martin was disheartened and slept very little.*
- *Next day, the fat day was waiting for Martin in the elevator. Frightened, Martin backed away from it. While the fat lady smiled at him as the elevator doors closed.*
- *In fear, Martin ran down the stairs but unfortunately tripped and fell. He broke his leg.*
- *Martin's father was angry at him for being foolish and didn't talk to him on the way to the hospital.*
- *On their way back, Martin felt relieved as his injury meant he didn't have to leave his apartment for a few days and as a consequence, he could avoid the fat lady.*

- In the elevator, his father suddenly remembered his promise to see Mrs. Ullman. To Martin's horror, he got off on the ninth floor leaving Martin alone.
- The fat lady got on the elevator on the tenth floor. Martin was too petrified and frozen to escape. He was too slow to move past her with his broken leg.
- The fat lady greeted Martin and laughed as she pushed the stop button.
- The story is written from a third person point of view and has an element of mystery and horror. The elevator and fat lady add an aura of something sinister as they fill Martin with terror.
- The character of the fat lady is the main element of horror as her description indicates that she wants something from Martin.
- The story is openended giving the freedom to the readers about Martin's fate-either he faces his fear or not. We do not necessarily know if Martin successfully gets out of the elevator.

Values Imparted

- At its core, 'The Elevator' is a meditation on the nature of fear and the power it holds over us.

Chapter 3 The Girl Who Can

Author: Ama Ata Aidoo

Setting

The story is set in a village in Ghana, Africa where the protagonist Adjoa lives with her Nana and mother. The story highlights the primitive society's perception of the role of a woman, being that of a child-bearer only.

Main Characters

Adjoa a 7 year old girl who struggles to express her thoughts and feelings.

Kaya Adjoa's supportive mother

Nana Adjoa's domineering grandmother, the matriarch of the household.

Theme

The themes of conflict, innocence, freedom, insecurity, connection and pride have been explored in the story.

Summary of the Chapter

- The Girl Who Can is a story about a seven year girl named Adjoa from a village Hasodzi, in Central Ghana. She lives with her mother, Maami (also called Kaya) and Nana, her mother's mother and the matriarch of the family.
- Adjoa struggles to voice her ideas in front of her traditional and authoritative Nana. She either gets laughed at by the elders or scolded to never repeat her opinions again. She feels discouraged and unheard at times.
- Nana often worries and complains about Adjoa's thin legs. She thought that all women need strong, meaty legs with good calves, as they support strong hips which in turn help in childbirth. The only exception she accepted were women without limbs.
- Maami would try to defend Adjoa but Nana would shut her up by shaming her for picking a bad life-partner.
- Annoyed by the regular argument, Adjoa often wished to see the legs of the women who had children. But she couldn't do so as the other women kept their legs wrapped and hidden all the time.
- School was another thing Nana disapproved of. She considered it a waste of time. Maami on the other hand, wished her daughter to learn, read, write and maybe calculate numbers. Her own inability to do so motivated her to send her daughter to school.
- One day, Adjoa, being a fast runner, is selected by her teachers to represent her school in district games for the junior section. Nana and Maami didn't believe it at first so Nana went to the school to confirm it.
- After the confirmation, they were pleased. Adjoa would often catch Nana staring at her legs with a strange look on her face but pretended otherwise.

- *She washed Adjoa's uniform herself and even borrowed Mr. Mensah's charcoal pressing iron to iron out the creases. She attended Adjoa's school parade and the district games in fresh old clothes.*
- *Adjoa wins every race and the title of best all-rounder junior athlete. Overjoyed, Nana carried the cup on her back like a baby all the way home. She proudly showed it to Maami before returning it to the headmaster.*
- *Nana cries softly as she is overwhelmed by happiness and accepts that thin legs can be useful to run and wonders what other uses they might have.*
- *Adjoa wonders the same but admits to not saying it out loud in fear of humiliation. But she is happy with the turn of events. Maami shows her approval with her usual silence.*
- *The story by Ama Ata. Aidoo sheds light on the complexities African women face in pursuing identity and fulfillment in male dominated societies. It presents the boundless potential of a girl to achieve something beyond societal expectations.*
- *The setting of the story is important as it presents the quest of a little girl Adjoa to understand the meaning of existence and a challenging environment. She represents progressive thinking and showcases the potential of women beyond traditional roles.*

Values Imparted

- Through the story, the author analyses the struggles of a woman to find her place in the society. The story imparts the lesson that a person, man or woman, can accomplish great things with determination and strong will.

Chapter 4 The Pedestrian

Author: Ray Bradbury

Setting

The setting of the story is 'a misty evening in November' in a large unnamed city. It is 8:00 pm and the year is A.D. 2053. In this city, everyone stays within their homes at night watching television.

Main Characters

The protagonist Mead, the only named character in the story, is an adult male living in an unnamed city in the middle of the 21st century.

Robotic Police Car The only other character besides Mead who speaks. It is revealed that the car is robotic and operated remotely.

Theme

The story deals with the themes of technology and dehumanisation, non-conformity and nature vs. the city.

Summary of the Chapter

- *The Pedestrian is a futurist dystopian story about a man Leonard Mead in 2053 A.D. and his experience one day on his regular evening walk.*
- *At eight o'clock on a misty November evening, Mr. Mead is out taking a stroll. He loved it a lot and would sometimes walk for hours. He would usually pass his neighbours' houses who were inside watching television. The streets felt as dead as a graveyard and the occasional shadows of the people felt like phantoms.*
- *His walks outside were unconventional as in this future technologically-driven society, people worked outside in the morning and spent the evening inside, addicted to the television shows.*
- *He decided to walk west towards the hidden sea. He walked noiselessly around the streets avoiding attention from the street dogs. He had learned from previous experience that his boots made loud noise against concrete and gathered attention. Thus, he switched to sneakers.*
- *He felt like a shadow of a lone hawk flying across midcountry, windless Arizona desert as he walked down the streets. Soon, he came across a clover intersection and decided to head home from there.*

- A block away from his home, a lone car suddenly approached him and flashed its light on him. The police car, in a cold metallic voice, asked him to stand still. When he protested, the car warned him to put his hand up or it would shoot.
- He was shocked to encounter another being outside on his walk for the first time in years. Ever since 2052, the police force cut down three patrol cars to one as the crime rates had dropped.
- The police car asked him his name and occupation. When he told him he is a writer, the police car interpreted it as no profession. He didn't correct them as he hadn't written anything in years. With the change in culture, the society preferred electronics over books.
- When the car asked him what he was doing out, he replied walking. They didn't believe his explanation. They couldn't understand why he would be outside at night walking aimlessly just 'for air and to see'. On being asked his marital status, he replied unmarried and joked that no one wanted him.
- After their questioning, the car ordered him to get inside the car. He protested but eventually obliged. On entering the car, he saw the car was empty as expected, indicating it was electronically controlled. The back seat of the car reminded him of a small cold jail with bars which smelled of riveted steel.
- The car told Mr. Mead that they were taking him to the Psychiatric Center for Research on Regressive Tendencies and he would have been saved if he had a wife to provide an alibi for him.
- On the way, the car passed his house. The house was the only one illuminated from the outside. When he remarked it was his house, he got no response. The car silently drove to its destination.
- Bradbury's story presents the dehumanising and ironically 'regressive' aspect of technology. In the world created by Bradbury, people were inclined towards technology such that even crime rates decreased and those like Mr. Mead are considered deviant by standards of society.
- Mr. Lead as such is a non-conforming writer whose life is set against the others, who are technology driven. His profession and act of walking to enjoy nature is almost criminal that he remains unmarried and is deemed mentally ill.

Values Imparted

- The story centres around the idea that, if mankind advances to the point where society loses its humanity, then it may as well cease to exist.

Chapter 5 The Last Lesson

Author: Alphonse Daudet

Setting

The story 'The Last Lesson' is set in the days of the Franco-Prussian War (1870-1871). The French districts of Alsace and Lorraine went into Prussian hands. The new Prussian rulers discontinued the teaching of French in the schools of these two districts.

Main Characters

Franz A school student (He is a sensitive and honest school boy who accepts his fault of ignoring his lessons.)

M. Hamel A teacher of French Language (He is a sincere and strict teacher of the French language who is passionately patriotic. He emerges as an epitome of an ideal teacher.)

Theme

A person's longing to learn their mother tongue. One's love for one's mother tongue.

Summary of the Chapter

- The Last Lesson is a story about a school boy Franz from a village in Alsace, France and his last French lesson.
- That morning, Franz was running late for M. Hamel's class. He forgot to learn his participles and feared scolding from his teacher. On his way to school, he passed town hall and saw a crowd in

front of the bulletin board. He was tempted to find out the current news but opted not to.

- *When he reached school, he found it oldly quieter than its usual hustle and bustle. When he entered, he expected scolding but M. Hamel surprised him with his kindness and asked him to quickly take his place.*
- *After settling, Franz noticed his teacher's fancy attire. M. Hamel was dressed in a beautiful green coat, frilled shirt and a little black embroidered silk cap. It was strange as he usually wore his fancy outfits for inspections and prize days. He also noticed the back benches that were usually empty were filled with village people. Everyone looked solemn.*
- *M. Hamel announced that it was his final class. Due to the annexation of Alsace and Lorriane into Germany, an order was passed to replace French with German. The new German teacher was to replace M. Hamel the next day.*
- *His teacher's declaration was like thunderclap to Franz. He understood why the crowd was outside the bulletin board. He realised that he hardly knew any French. He was suddenly very regretful for chasing birds' eggs instead of paying attention in his classes. He understood why his teacher was dressed in his best clothes and the presence of the village elders. They wanted to thank M. Hamel for the forty years of service he provided to their village.*
- *Franz wanted to recite his reading perfectly but couldn't. Ashamed he stood in the class awaiting his teacher's fury. Instead, M. Hamel consoled him. He remarked how everyone in the village, including himself, took education lightly. M. Hamel pointed out that they all had procrastinated and prioritised other tasks, taking their freedom and learning for granted. He repented how the Prussians will have the right to mock them for calling themselves Frenchmen but not knowing their own language and culture.*
- *He also talked about the beauty of the French language. He urged everyone to never forget it and guard it as it was their key to freedom.*
- *The class went from reading to grammar. Franz was astonished by how well he understood his lesson that day. The lesson in writing followed. M. Hamel got new copies for everyone. He wrote 'France, Alsace, France, Alsace' with a beautiful round hand on top of them. It looked like little flags floating on top of their desks. The class worked diligently on their lesson. Even the young ones traced their fish hooks as if they were French.*
- *Meanwhile M. Hamel sat lost and motionless in his chair, trying to memorise every detail of the place. Upstairs, his sister was packing as they were leaving the country next day.*
- *When the clock struck twelve, the trumpets from the Prussians returning from the drill could be heard outside the window. M. hamel got tongue-tied from all the emotions and wrote 'Viva La France' in large words on the blackboard. He asked the class to leave as the school was now dismissed.*
- *Daudet's story explores the effects of cultural subjugation in the time of war. It presents how language becomes a means of control. At the same time, the story, also points out how with language, one can assert ones love for the country and gain freedom.*

Values Imparted

- Patriotism and the importance of the mother tongue.

i Succeed
Sample Question Papers

Quick Study Notes

Poetry

Poetry

Chapter I Haunted Houses

Poet: H.W. Longfellow

Setting

The poems setting—a deserted, dilapidated house—serves as a powerful metaphor for the passage of time.

Theme

The central theme of the poem is the relentless passage of time.

Summary of the Poem

- Longfellow's poem considers the paranormal elements to be harmless. He believes that humans are residing in houses that are haunted. He claims that these spirits who have left Earth still exist in their previous residences.
- These ghosts are crowded everywhere in these houses. Even though they are unseen, their presence may be sensed as they move through the house's passageways.
- They are as silent and innocent as the wall images. They don't create any noise or disturb anyone. The poet is delighted to have them join the other guests at the table.
- The poet is the only one who can sense or perceive their presence.
- The poet claims that these ghosts of the previous house owners no longer possess the 'house' and have no 'property deals'. They are unaffected by materialistic pleasures and lack worldly ambitions. Saying this, he hints at human's desire for materialistic possessions. However, the poet asserts that even the living cannot claim anything to be perpetually theirs.
- The poet establishes a connection between physical and spiritual realms. He believes they coexist. The spiritual realm is like an 'atmosphere' that floats around the Earth. Mist and vapour form the passage between the two realms.
- The poet compares human's desires spiritual contentment. Humans are never at peace and constantly try to rise above and achieve greatness. This brings meaning and happiness to one's life. He also talks about the influence of celestial bodies over human nature. Humans are greedy and their wants and curiosity never end. Spirits however have no such ambitions and live in peace.
- Moon has always been considered a mysterious object. The opening in the clouds is considered as 'a dark gate'. The moonlight that illuminates the sea surface appears as a floating bridge. The poet imagines this unsteady bridge to act as a passage for the souls to travel between realms.
- The poet also argues that the spirits have a lingering effect in our lives. They hold memories of our past and our loved ones that remain with us forever.
- For the poem 'haunted' is not horror but a harmless presence.
- Through the poem, the poet points out the need balance earthly wants and high aspirations.

Values Imparted

- The poem invites contemplation on the significance of memories and the emotional resonance of places tied to our past.

Chapter 2 The Glove and the Lions

Poet: Leigh Hunt

Setting

The poem is set in the royal court of King Francis, where nobles and ladies gather to witness a spectacle of valour and love.

Main Characters

King Francis a lively, vigorous and energetic king who took delight in royal sports.

Count de Lorge a brave Count who only had eyes for one lady and proved his love for her.

The Counts Lady Love a beautiful and confident lady whose vanity cost her the Count's love.

Theme

The poem deals with the theme of bravery and chivalry and vanity.

Summary of the Poem

- *Strong-willed and a fan of royal sports, King Frances enjoyed seeing lions compete. One day, he had noblemen with their ladies come and watch the lions fight. The spectacle was magnificent, worthy of the most illustrious nobility.*
- *Count de Lorge and his lady love were among the noblemen. She had a vibrant, attractive smile on her lips and bright eyes that never failed to catch the attention.*
- *The lions fought fiercely. They scowled, bit and charged with such force that it appeared as though the wind was blowing. They roared and rolled around, crashing into one other until the sand in the pit merged in with their manes like a dense cloud. A froth of blood flew above the barriers surrounding the pit. This is also the poet's comment about noblemen fighting each other to gain the King's favour.*
- *The king joked that it was good that the people were outside the pit, away from the ferocious lions. De Lorge's sweetheart overheard the King's comment. She thought the Count was courageous and would go to great lengths to show her how much he cared. In order to claim the honour of a courageous lover, she made the decision to throw her glove into the lions' pit for him to retrieve.*
- *She let go of her glove, grinned and looked at the Count expectantly. He bowed, darted between the pack of lions and swiftly grabbed the glove. He came back to his place and threw the glove at her face.*
- *The King commended the Count for his deed. However, the Count was unhappy because the lady's actions were motivated by conceit rather than love.*
- *The lighthearted melody like poem presents the central plot of a love story between the Count and his lady.*

Values Imparted

- Pride and vanity are not acceptable in any society. One should be humble and polite in all situations.

Chapter 3 When Great Trees fall

Poet: Maya Angelou

Theme

The poem depicts how the speaker feels grief because of the loss of a loved one.

Summary of the Poem

- *The poem conveys the deep effect of loss on the living by drawing a long metaphor which compares the fall of trees and the death of great individuals.*
- *The poet portrays the aftermath of a large tree falling. In the natural world, this seemingly solitary event of a tree falling has a significant impact and the incident has a ripple effect. Elephants seek refuge, lions seek cover and distant rocks tremble. The smaller creatures go silent, either from terror or from the abrupt change in their surroundings numbing their senses. This captures the instant silence and astonishment that frequently accompany a tragic incident.*
- *The poem shifts from talking about actual trees to symbolic ones, and laments the passing of great souls-people who have had a profound influence on others. The air appears lighter, rarer and more sterile after they are gone. People find difficulty in breathing, their vision blurred as they remember painful memories and they feel regret for unfulfilled plans and they feel words that remained unsaid.*
- *The poet suggests that the presence of these great souls is entwined with our reality. Their departure causes us to become less of who we are – we feel lost. Our souls shrink and our thoughts lose the light of their guidance.*
- *The poem ends on a note of healing. After a period of time, tranquility and positive energy replace the vacuum left by the loss. As we adjust to the new reality, our senses serve as a reminder that these great souls were once among us. Their existence enabled us to be ourselves and to strive to be better.*
- *Overall, the poem captures the complicated and transformative nature of grief as we move through the stages of shock, mourning, loss of self, acceptance and inspiration after a great loss.*

Values Imparted

- The poem implies that 'great souls'—the most impressive or talented people in a given community—have an outsized impact on the world around them. Both in life and death, they reshape their entire culture, just as the flourishing or toppling of a huge tree can nurture or shake up an entire landscape.

Chapter 4 A Considerable Speck

Poet: Robert Frost

Setting

The poem captures an encounter between a poet and a tiny creature on a blank sheet of paper.

Theme

The poem is a fascinating meditation on the theme of intelligence, consciousness and the value of even the smallest forms of life.

Summary of the Poem

- *The poem is a reflection on the value of the human capacity for creativity and thought. It makes fun of those who lack consciousness and are too dull to take action.*
- *The poet discovers a particle an insect on his paper while writing. He realises it's a 'living mite,' and decides to kill it with his pen.*
- *The mite, sensing danger, turns to the opposite side of the paper. There it encounters a wet drop of ink. It hesitates to smell or taste the ink and realises it is also bad. It runs again in another direction. It eventually appears to give up and acknowledge that it is at the mercy of a higher power-the poet. It comes to a stop and squats in the center of the page.*

- *The poet realises that he is undoubtedly working with an intelligent mite. He is deeply moved by the sight and leaves it to lie there. He hopes that it will fall asleep.*
- *The poet realises that he lacks the contemporary world's 'tenderer-than-thou' collectivist mindset, which loves to ruin everything that they think is inferior to them. He chooses to leave the mite alone because it has proved itself harmless. He respects the mite for having his own mind unlike the mindless people who are too drab to act when required.*
- *The mite, despite its tiny size and lack of significance, possesses the ability to alter the poet's perspective and gain his respect. The poet also draws attention to the mite's battles for survival, implying that even the tiniest animals are capable of consciousness and reasoning.*

Values Imparted

- The poem presents an interesting perspective on mindfulness and awareness in everyday life. The poem describes the poets observation of a tiny speck on his manuscript, which he eventually realises is a living creature.

Chapter 5 The Power of Music

Poet: Sukumar Ray

Main Characters
Bhisma Lochan Sharma His singing is energetic and intense and his voice spreads from Delhi to Burma.

Theme
The poem deals with the themes of persistence and obliviousness.

Summary of the Poem

- *The poem recounts a hilarious and dramatic story about Bhisma Lochan Sharma singing.*
- *The songs of Bhisma Lochan Sharma can be heard in the summertime across plains and hills stretching from Delhi to Burma. He sings with all of his might, as if his life depended on it.*
- *The people are exhausted by his forceful singing even if they are aware of his good intentions. A stampede or sickness occurs in response to the sound of his song. They beg Bhisma to cease his singing but he doesn't.*
- *Animals are miserable and detest the sound as soon as they hear it. They cry out, fidget and even raise their feet in a bewildered manner. The bullock carts upturn and horses stop beside the road, but the passionate vocalist is unaffected.*
- *Trees quake and collapse with a boom that can be heard a mile away. Fish dive deeper in search of peace. Birds in the sky turn over on their backs. His high-pitched singing causes the sky to cry. The imposing, lofty houses fall. People beg Bhisma again to stop singing as they might scream and die, but to no avail. Bhisma's voice rises over the cries of the grieving or pleading.*
- *One day, a smart billy goat appears. In response to the booming voice of Bhisma, it lowered its head and charged. He head-butts the singer, and tosses him around till the singing ends.*
- *Bhisma Lochan Sharma is finally quiet, a golden gift to everyone around him.*
- *Through the poem, Ray employs satire to mock the societal norms and pretentiousness of those who persist in their endeavours despite lack of talent. The chaos of Bhisma's continuous singing presents the absurdity of his persistence and misplaced confidence.*
- *Interestingly, the goat seems to represent common sense or force of nature that strives to bring sanity and order.*

Values Imparted

- The poem conveys a message of using musical talents wisely.

i Succeed

Sample Question Papers

Quick Study Notes

Drama

Drama

Julius Caesar

Author: William Shakespeare

Setting

The play *Julius Caesar* is based in Rome during the First Century BC, during the last days of the life of Julius Caesar. During this time, Rome was undergoing a great deal of friction between the wealthy and the poor, with the poor throwing much of their support to Julius Caesar.

Main Characters

Julius Caesar A powerful Roman general and politician, assassinated by a group of conspirators.

Marcus Brutus A noble Roman senator and close friend of Caesar, who is persuaded to join the conspiracy against him.

Caius Cassius A cunning politician who manipulates Brutus to join the conspiracy.

Mark Antony A loyal friend and supporter of Caesar who seeks revenge for his murder.

Calpurnia Caesar's wife, who has bad omens about the day of his assassination.

Theme

The play deals with the themes of fate vs. free will, honour vs. ambition, tyranny and power.

ACT III SCENE I

- Artemidorus and the Soothsayer await Caesar in the street. Caesar enters with Brutus, Cassius, Casca, Decius, Metellus, Trebonius, Cinna, Ligarius, Antony and other senators.
- Artemidorus approaches Caesar with his letter, saying that its contents are a matter of concern for him. Caesar dismisses him and decides to address personal concerns later.
- As they enter the Senate, Cassius fears the assassination plot has been uncovered.
- Trebonius draws Antony away from the Senate room.
- Metellus approaches Caesar to plead his brother Publius Cimber be granted permission to return to Rome. Caesar refuses and states that Publius was banished lawfully. Brutus and Cassius kneel in front of him but Caesar declares his decision to be as constant as the Northern star.
- Cinna kneels in front of Caesar followed by Decius, Ligarius and finally Casca. Casca then stabs Caesar first and others follow. The last blow is done by Brutus, and after realising Brutus's involvement, Caesar submits and dies.
- Conspirators rejoice and other members leave in turmoil. Trebonius announces that Antony fled.
- Brutus urges everyone to bathe their hands in Caesar's blood and walk the streets to Rome to proclaim freedom and peace. Cassius agrees with him.
- Antony sends a message to Brutus through his servant. He writes of his sadness on Caesar's demise but vows to serve Brutus if the latter doesn't punish him for his former loyalties. Brutus promises to not harm Antony. He justifies his decision to Cassius who disagrees with him.
- Antony arrives and sees Caesar's corpse and wonders how such a great man can end in such a small body. He urges the conspirators to kill him if they wish as he would not mind dying beside Caesar. Brutus denies his request. He declares that their actions may appear terrible but it was done out of their love and devotion towards the Roman people. Antony accepts his explanation and shakes the bloody hands of all the conspirators. He stains Trebonius's hands in the process as they were unstained from not being on the scene.
- Antony asks for forgiveness with Caesar's soul for joining hands with the conspirators. He praises

Caesar which makes Cassius question his loyalty. Antony assures him of his allegiance and that his words were just an emotional response. He pledges to be their friend as long as the conspirators can justify the reason behind Caesar's assassination. Brutus ensures Antony that he would find the reason just and satisfactory.

- Antony pleads the chance to speak at Caesar's funeral. Cassius disagrees as he is still suspicious of Antony's motives and fears his speech would lead the crowd to mutiny. Brutus dismisses his concerns and grants Antony permission to speak as long as he doesn't speak ill of the conspirators. Brutus also reveals his plan to preface Antony's speech. He allows Antony to take Caesar's body with him.
- After everyone leaves, Antony expresses his real intentions in front of Caesar's dead body. He asks Caesar for forgiveness for playing nice with the conspirators. He vows to avenge his death and that Caesar's spirit will evoke civil war and destruction of Rome.
- Octavius's servant sees Caesar's body with Antony. Antony commands him to return to his master and keep him out of the city for now as Rome is currently dangerous for him. Antony wanted to see the crowd's reaction to his speech before he could plan his next steps. He also asks the servant to return to listen to his speech.

ACT III SCENE 2

- The plebians arrive in Rome's Forum. A portion of it follows Cassius, others stay to hear Brutus.
- Brutus justifies assassinating Caesar. He begs to be taken seriously, citing his honour as justification. He asserts that his love for Caesar was equal to that of any of his friends, but his passion for Rome outweighed his love for Caesar.
- Despite being pleased with Caesar's achievements, he assassinated him for Caesar's ambition. He says that he has angered only those who do not abhor bondage and he invites them to speak up.
- Brutus backs off, allowing Antony to continue. The crowd, impressed with Brutus, praises him.
- Antony starts with saying that the good deeds of men are forgotten when they are buried, while their misdeeds are remembered. He agrees that Caesar was ambitious but also his friend. He addresses Brutus as an 'honourable man' from this point on.
- According to Antony, Caesar was a conqueror who stuffed Rome's coffers but also cried with the underprivileged and turned down the throne three times.
- The crowd begins to shift. Antony says he doesn't want to incite a mutiny as he would be wronging Brutus and others, and would instead choose to wrong a deceased person over such honourable men.
- He subtly points out that they (the crowd) were Caesar's descendants and he doesn't want to reveal how much Caesar loved them for fear that it would incite them.
- By this point, the crowd has formed a circle around Caesar's corpse. Antony evokes memories of Caesar's grandeur by bringing up his cloak which was once noble and now soaked in his blood.
- He subtly singled out Brutus and presented how his betrayal devastated Caesar's heart. This stirs up the mob. Antony begs for calmness.
- He declares that he is not as good a speaker as Brutus. He claims to be a straightforward individual who adores Caesar and subtly expresses provocative sentiments that encourage rebellion. He, then, reads Caesar's will and reveals that Caesar had left his personal gardens and some of his wealth to the people of Rome.
- The mob, enraged, prepares to honour Caesar and vows to set fire to the traitors' homes.
- Lepidus and Octavius Caesar arrive in Rome. Antony is happy with the aftermath of his speech. He is even more ecstatic after learning that Cassius and Brutus have fled Rome.

ACT III SCENE 3

- The poet Cinna is confronted by a group of rowdy residents while travelling to attend Caesar's burial. They enquire who he is and where he is going.
- Cinna is completely perplexed by the bombardment of questions from the crowd. They beg him to immediately respond to them. He introduces himself as Cinna and says he's headed to Caesar's burial.

- They approach to attack him, thinking he's Cinna, the conspirator. He begs to be believed as Cinna the poet but they respond that poor poetry will get him killed anyhow.
- The mob proceeds to beat him to death. They then yell out the names of the conspirators whose homes they want to loot and set on fire.

ACT IV SCENE I

- Antony, Lepidus, and Octavius plan to make the second triumvirate of Rome.
- They gather in Antony's home to list the conspirators that should be killed. Lepidus consents to his brother's death, and Antony consents to the death of his nephew.
- Antony then dispatches Lepidus to get a copy of Caesar's will to lessen some of the bequests.
- After Lepidus leaves, Antony informs Octavius that while Lepidus might be able to conduct errands, he is not fit to rule with them. He reveals his intentions of utilising him and his resources; and eventually take over his power. He also plans to use him as scapegoat for all his misdeeds in the future.
- Octavius disagrees with Antony and claims to trust Lepidus. He believes Lepidus to be a seasoned and brave soldier. However Antony says, 'So is my horse,' in response. He continues to characterise Lepidus as a tool or a simple animal.
- Seeing Octavius's disagreement, Antony shifts the focus of the conversation to Brutus and Cassius, who are assembling an army.
- Antony reminds Octavius that it's up to them to confront them and put an end to their attempt at seizing power. He urges the need to organise the troops and battle strategies.

ACT IV SCENE 2

- The scene takes place in Sardis, outside of Rome.
- After recruiting forces in different Roman provinces, Cassius and Brutus now meet at Brutus's camp at Sardis. They intend to join forces against Antony and Octavius.
- Prior to Cassius' arrival, Titinius and Pindarus arrive at the camp. Lucilius also arrives after visiting Cassius. Titinius and Pindarus are informed by Brutus about his disapproval of some of their lord's actions and wishes it could be undone. Pindarus assures Brutus of his master's actions and that he is closeby to answer his questions.
- Lucilius brings a letter for Brutus from Cassius. Brutus pulls him aside to inquire about his reception. When Lucilius informs him of Cassius' cold and formal behaviour, Brutus insults Cassius by calling him a deceitful jade and a 'hot friend cooling.'
- Cassius approaches Brutus and accuses him of transgressions. Brutus claims he would never harm his enemies, much less a friend he considers to be a brother.
- He emphasises the need of putting up a united front and tells Cassius to remain calm in front of soldiers. Brutus offers his tent to provide privacy for their conversation.

ACT IV SCENE 3

- Inside the tent, Cassius complains to Brutus for denouncing Lucilius for accepting bribes and his disregard to Cassius's letters in favour of Lucius Pella. Cassius argues that such offenses should be forgiven in the current situation.
- Brutus disagrees. Brutus accuses Cassius for being greedy and accepting bribes. Cassius becomes quite offended. Brutus warns Cassius that Caesar was slain for the sake of justice and for not punishing robbers.
- Cassius reminds Brutus that he is older, more seasoned and that Brutus cannot dominate him.
- The two yell abusive and furious remarks at one other. Though Brutus hypocritically demands the gold that Cassius refused to provide, Cassius asserts that the messenger misrepresented the situation.
- Cassius yells that he is sick of the world because the one he loves despises him. He pulls out his dagger, but Brutus advises him to focus his rage where it's needed.
- Cassius learns that Brutus's wife Portia committed suicide by swallowing burning coal after learning Antony and Octavius have teamed together. Brutus appears numb and doesn't show emotion.
- Brutus and Messala discuss the letters that tell them that several senators, including Cicero, have been executed by Octavius and Antony. When Messala tells Brutus of Portia's passing, Brutus doesn't lose his composure.

- *Regarding whether to march to the Philippi, Cassius and Brutus argue. Cassius wishes to remain where they are. Brutus counters by saying that the plebeians will swell the opposing forces.*
- *As they tell each other good night, Brutus requests Varro and Claudius to stay with him in case he has messages for Cassius. Lucilius plays a tune till he falls asleep.*
- *As Brutus opens his book, the ghost of Caesar walks in. The ghost tells Brutus that he will see him at Philippi and disappears.*
- *Brutus, shaken from the encounter, awakens Varro and Claudius to ask why they cried out in their sleep. The two respond confused as they are unaware of crying or seeing anything.*
- *Brutus decides to leave for Philippi immediately and leaves a message for Cassius to follow him in the morning.*

ACT V SCENE 1

- *Antony and Octavius Caesar arrive in the Philippi with their forces. The adversary, Brutus and Cassius, are also prepared for combat.*
- *The more seasoned soldier, Antony, orders Octavius to launch an attack from the left side of the field. But, Octavius declines and asserts that he would attack from the right, leaving left for Antony.*
- *The opposing generals gather in the middle of the field to converse first. The two sides start insulting one other right away.*
- *Antony calls Brutus out for his seeming duplicity in the assassination, and he mocks the conspirators for their cowardly method of killing Caesar. Cassius charges Antony of lying to the conspirators after the killing, and tells Brutus that if Antony had perished with Caesar, they wouldn't have to put up with his nasty remarks today.*
- *Cassius makes fun of Octavius' youth and Antony's reputation for partying. Reaching no resolve, Antony and Octavius depart back to their forces.*
- *Cassius informs Messala that he saw crows and ravens soar through the air, creating shadows across the battlefields. Cassius believes the scavenger birds as omen of defeat for their army. Still, he declares that he is prepared for battle.*
- *Brutus and Cassius say their final goodbyes. Brutus announces his intentions to accept his fate. But he declines to go back to Rome as a slave.*
- *Cassius and Brutus are marching towards the battleground with their forces.*

ACT V SCENE 2

- *Brutus dispatches Messala to order Cassius to immediately confront the enemy army.*
- *The forces under Octavius, who are positioned in front of him, seem upset and vulnerable, in Brutus' opinion. He feels that Octavius' army has a weakness.*
- *He orders Cassius to attack Antony's forces immediately so they are in no shape to aid Octavius' troops.*
- *He prematurely attacks without waiting for Cassius to attack.*

ACT V SCENE 3

- *Cassius observes his soldiers pulling back in the battlefield. For his cowardice, he murders his standard bearer.*
- *Titinius believes that Brutus gave the order too soon. Pindarus informs Cassius that Antony has infiltrated Cassius's camp. When Cassius notices the tents are on fire, he sends Titinius to determine if the soldiers inside are allies or enemies. He gives Pindarus the order to ascend the hill and inform him of what transpires.*
- *According to Pindarus, Titinius is encircled and being held captive. Cassius is disheartened.*
- *Cassius reminds Pindarus of his time in Parthia and how he safeguarded his life in exchange for a favour from Pindarus. Cassius requests that Pindarus stab him with his own sword.*
- *Pindarus bound to his promise complies with Cassius' wishes. He stabs him and departs in grief, hoping to escape the Romans.*
- *Titinius returns with Messala. According to the Messala, Brutus has defeated Octavius. They find Cassius's corpse on the ground. Messala realises that despair leads people to do horrible things. Cassius had doubted his chances of achievement and passed away in misery.*

- *Titinius regrets that Cassius misinterpreted the triumphant allies welcoming him. He kills himself after placing the wreath of victory on Cassius's brow.*
- *Brutus enters with others searching for Cassius's body. He exclaims that Caesar's curse is making them kill themselves. Although he laments, Brutus promises to take time to properly mourn his friend. He gives the order to send Cassius's corpse to Thaos and the rest of his troops to prepare for another battle.*

ACT V SCENE 4

- *While everyone is fighting, Brutus arrives with Cato, Lucilius, and other people.*
- *He commands them to take a stance and fight valiantly. They ought to issue the adversary with a strong challenge. Saying this, Brutus leaves.*
- *Young Cato declares his allegiance to Rome but gets killed by the enemy troops.*
- *The enemy soldiers mistake Lucilius for Brutus, so they take him prisoner. Upon Antony's arrival, Lucilius informs him that Brutus is still alive and safe and will never be taken hostage.*
- *Antony, impressed by Lucilius's loyalty, asks his men to treat him like a friend. He sends his warriors to find Brutus - dead or alive.*

ACT V SCENE 5

- *Brutus arrives with a group of his friends. They are weary of fighting.*
- *First, he asks Clitus to kill him, and then Dardanius. Neither of them comply.*
- *He tells Volumnius that he has seen Caesar's ghost once more on the battlefield and that he is aware that his time is running out.*
- *Brutus is urged by all three to keep escaping the enemies, but he refuses and says goodbye to them all. Volumnius feels that killing his companion was wrong.*
- *At last, Brutus requests Strato to hold the blade while he runs across it. Strato complies with Brutus. Brutus kills himself and asks Caesar's ghost to rest now.*
- *Antony, Octavius, Messala, Lucilius, and other troops enter. Octavius and Antony have taken Messala and Lucilius as captives. They find Strato holding the lifeless body of Brutus who explains to them of Brutus's plight.*
- *Antony proclaims that among all the conspirators who had banded together to assassinate the great Caesar, Brutus was the most noble. The other conspirators murdered Caesar out of jealousy and personal grudges. However, Brutus had entered the plot with a noble intent, for the wellbeing of all Romans.*
- *Antony gives Brutus a heartfelt homage. Octavius declares that Brutus will be buried like a military grave with honour. In addition, he suggests that everyone depart from the arena and celebrate their victories on this joyous day.*

Values Imparted

- The moral of the play centers on murder as an acceptable means of political power. Conspirators plot against Caesar and justify their actions as honourable claiming that Caesar's assassination is for the greater good of Rome. However, murder cannot be justified, especially in the context of an assassination. In the end, Caesar's assassination is avenged by Mark Antony demonstrating that murder is not an acceptable means to gain power.